The Sure Mercies Of David

A Story of God's Mercy

Clifford Brant Beaver

The Sure Mercies of David
A Story of God's Mercy

ISBN: 979-8-9903038-4-3

All Scripture references are from the King James Version Bible

The Holy Bible, King James Version. Cambridge Edition: 1769; *King James Bible Online*, 2024. www.kingjamesbibleonline.org.

Some scripture is underlined and/or emboldened. This is done to emphasize certain words or phrases although it is not in the original text.

This Book is Dedicated to Valerie, Isabel, and Carter

Table of Contents

The Sure Mercies of David

The Sure Mercies of David

The Sure Mercies of David is about the Eternal Security of the Believer. There are arguments among Christians regarding whether a person who has been Born Again is Eternally Secure or if they can lose their Salvation. The purpose of this book is to show you what the Bible says about Salvation and Eternal Security. There is nothing that will give you more peace than knowing beyond a doubt that Heaven is your home.

Christ the Son of David

There was once a man named David who was King of Israel. David was the son of Jesse, who was from Bethlehem, and who was of the tribe of Judah. David held a special place in God's heart and God even stated that David was a man who had a heart that was like God's heart. David was a man of honour and dignity. He trusted in the Lord with all his heart. He was a loyal friend, and he was a great warrior. David was also a shepherd of sheep. He was a good shepherd who put his own life at risk to defend his sheep. A lion and a bear once tried to kill his sheep and he fought them off and killed them. God esteemed David so much that He decided that Israel's Messiah-The Christ would be born as a descendant of David.

God told David that he was going to die and go to the place where his ancestors were. However, He also told David that He was going to anoint one of David's descendants to be King, and the Kingdom of this Descendant would last forever!

> 1 Chronicles 17:11 And it shall come to pass, when thy days be expired that thou must go to be with thy fathers, that I will raise up thy seed after thee, which shall be of thy sons; and I will establish his kingdom.

God says that this Son is going to build Him a house. Many people think that God was referring to Solomon here and the temple that Solomon built. Solomon became king after David died. There's also a scripture that shows that even David thought this would be fulfilled with Solomon. However, we'll see that this scripture didn't find its ultimate fulfillment in Solomon.

> 1 Chronicles 17:12 <u>He shall build me an house</u>, and I will stablish his throne for ever.

God goes on to say that this coming King is going to be His son. This is a special title. God loved David and David held a very special place in God's heart, but even David was never referred to as God's son. He also tells David that He won't take away His mercy from Him. This is in contrast to how God took His mercy away from Saul who was king before David. Saul didn't obey God, and as a result, God took the Kingdom of Israel away from Saul and gave it to David.

> 1 Chronicles 17:13 **I will be his father, and he shall be my son**: and I will not take my mercy away from him, as I took it from him that was before thee:
>
> 1 Chronicles 17:14 But I will settle him in mine house and in my kingdom for ever: and **his throne shall be established for evermore**.

So, King David died and Solomon, who was one of David's sons, became king in his place. Solomon also held a special place in God's heart. As a matter of fact, God blessed Solomon in a very special way. God gave Solomon wisdom and made him wiser than any man on the earth. He also made Solomon richer than any man on earth. The Kingdom of Israel was in the height of its power during the reign of Solomon and Solomon built the first Temple. Before the Temple, the sacrifices and offerings had been done in a Tabernacle which resembled a large tent.

It seemed as if God's promises to David were being fulfilled in Solomon's life and in his reign. However, Solomon in all his wisdom was still just a man, and like any other man, Solomon wasn't perfect. Solomon had a ton of wives, many of whom came from other kingdoms, and many of them didn't serve the True God. Eventually, Solomon gave in to the request of some of his wives who wanted to set up altars to false gods. This angered God and God judged Solomon's Kingdom. After Solomon died, his son Rehoboam became king. During the reign of Rehoboam, God allowed a rift to happen between Rehoboam and the people which led to the Kingdom of Israel being divided. In fact, the majority of Israel followed a man named Jeroboam. Only the tribes of Judah and Benjamin remained loyal to Rehoboam. The Kingdom of Israel that seemed so glorious under Solomon was gone and instead, there were two lesser kingdoms, which were the Kingdom of Israel and the Kingdom of Judah.

Many years passed and both the Kingdoms of Israel and Judah had problems. They even went to war against each other at times which involved hundreds of thousands of casualties. Judah for the most part remained more loyal to God than Israel, and the kings of Judah all remained in David's bloodline. In contrast, the Kingdom of Israel had kings from different bloodlines and different tribes. The Kingdom of Israel worshipped other gods and was eventually taken away by the Assyrians so that only the Kingdom of Judah remained. Sadly, not too long after that, Judah was conquered by Babylon. Most of Judah's people were taken away and Solomon's Temple was destroyed. The Kingdom that started with David had come to an end. You see, God tells us that anything a man builds will come to an end. For something to last forever, it must be built by God.

> Psalm 127:1 **Except the LORD build the house, they labour in vain that build it**: except the LORD keep the city, the watchman waketh but in vain.

Although David's Kingdom was gone, his bloodline remained. The descendants of the Kings of Judah went to Babylon, but eventually through miraculous circumstances, they came back to the land of Israel. The Prophets prophesied about the Branch who would come. The Branch would be a direct descendant of King David.

> Isaiah 11:1 And there shall come forth a rod out of the stem of Jesse, and a **Branch** shall grow out of his roots:
>
> Zechariah 3:8 Hear now, O Joshua the high priest, thou, and thy fellows that sit before thee: for they are men wondered at: for, behold, **I will bring forth my servant the BRANCH.**

The Prophet Jeremiah also prophesied about the Branch. Jeremiah told us that the Branch would be King and that He would execute judgment and justice in the earth. Jeremiah also says that the name of the Branch would be "THE LORD OUR RIGHTEOUSNESS"!

> Jeremiah 23:5 Behold, the days come, saith the LORD, that I will raise unto David a righteous **Branch**, and a King shall reign and prosper, and shall execute judgment and justice in the earth.
>
> Jeremiah 23:6 In his days Judah shall be saved, and Israel shall dwell safely: and this is his name whereby he shall be called, THE LORD OUR RIGHTEOUSNESS.

Remember when God told David that his Descendant would build Him a house? It seemed like this was fulfilled when Solomon built the Temple but remember Solomon's Temple didn't last. Well, Zechariah prophesied that the Branch would build God's Temple!

> Zechariah 6:12 And speak unto him, saying, Thus speaketh the LORD of hosts, saying, Behold the man whose name is **The BRANCH**; and he shall grow up out of his place, **and he shall build the temple of the LORD:**

If everything a man builds will eventually perish, what would make the Branch's Temple or His Kingdom last forever? If the Branch's Temple is going to last forever and if His Kingdom is going to last forever, the Branch must be God! Isaiah told us that the Son who was going to be given to Israel and who would sit on David's throne would be the Mighty God!

> Isaiah 9:6 For unto us a child is born, <u>unto us a son is given</u>: and the government shall be upon his shoulder: and **his name shall be called** Wonderful, Counsellor, **The mighty God**, The everlasting Father, The Prince of Peace.
>
> Isaiah 9:7 Of the increase of his government and peace there shall be no end, **upon the throne of David**, and upon his kingdom, to order it, and to establish it with judgment and with justice from henceforth even for ever. The zeal of the LORD of hosts will perform this.

The Branch is none other than Jesus Christ. Jesus is the Son of God who is God in human form, and He is also the Son of David who was promised to come from David. The writer of Hebrews shows us that God was referring to Jesus all along when He made His promise to David.

Hebrews 1:5 For unto which of the angels said he at any time, Thou art my Son, this day have I begotten thee? And again, **I will be to him a Father, and he shall be to me a Son?**	1 Chronicles 17:13 **I will be his father, and he shall be my son**: and I will not take my mercy away from him, as I took it from him that was before thee:

When Jesus was on the earth there were of course people that recognized Him as the Christ. A lot of them also understood that Christ was the Son of David who was promised to come to them. There was once a blind man who begged Jesus to help him. He called Jesus the Son of David as he asked for mercy.

> Mark 10:47 And when he heard that it was Jesus of Nazareth, he began to cry out, and say, **Jesus, thou son of David**, have mercy on me.

8

When Jesus rode into Jerusalem there were people who cried Hosanna. Hosanna basically means "Savior please save us".

> Matthew 21:9 And the multitudes that went before, and that followed, cried, saying, **Hosanna to the son of David**: Blessed is he that cometh in the name of the Lord; Hosanna in the highest.

Also, notice that after they cry "Hosanna to the son of David" they say, "Blessed is he that cometh in the name of the Lord". The reason they are saying this is because they recognize that Jesus is the Lord who was sent to save them, and they are quoting from God's promises in Psalm 118.

> Psalm 118:25 **Save now, I beseech thee, O LORD**: O LORD, I beseech thee, send now prosperity.
> Psalm 118:26 **Blessed be he that cometh in the name of the LORD**: we have blessed you out of the house of the LORD.

Of course, as we've already established, this Lord who comes to save is God.

> Psalm 118:27 **God is the LORD**, which hath shewed us light: bind the sacrifice with cords, even unto the horns of the altar.

Only when the Holy Ghost gives you understanding will you fully understand that Jesus is the Lord and He is God. Jesus is not A Lord, He is THE LORD, THE LORD OF LORDS AND KING OF KINGS.

> 1 Corinthians 12:3 Wherefore I give you to understand, that no man speaking by the Spirit of God calleth Jesus accursed: and that no man can say that **Jesus is the Lord**, but by the Holy Ghost.

Jesus the Son of God came to earth to save us. He also came to build His Temple. Some of the Jews once asked Jesus to show them a sign. He was at the Temple (not Solomon's Temple but the rebuilt one) when they had this conversation with Him. Jesus told them the sign would be that they would destroy the Temple but that He'd raise it up in three days.

> John 2:19 Jesus answered and said unto them, Destroy this temple, and in three days I will raise it up.

The Jews didn't understand how a physical Temple could be built in three days when the one that was standing took 46 years to build.

> John 2:20 Then said the Jews, Forty and six years was this temple in building, and wilt thou rear it up in three days?

But Jesus wasn't referring to a physical Temple. He was referring to His body. You see, a Temple is a place where God's Spirit dwells. God never wanted a Temple of rocks and wood made by a man. He's always wanted to dwell inside of His people.

> John 2:21 But he spake of the temple of his body.
> John 2:22 When therefore he was risen from the dead, his disciples remembered that he had said this unto them; and they believed the scripture, and the word which Jesus had said.

Jesus is the Cornerstone of God's Temple. He is the first stone. Born Again believers make up the rest of the Temple. We are also members of the Body of Christ which is the whole of the Temple.

> Ephesians 2:20 And are built upon the foundation of the apostles and prophets, **Jesus Christ himself being the chief corner stone**;
> Ephesians 2:21 In whom all the building fitly framed together groweth unto **an holy temple in the Lord**:
> Ephesians 2:22 **In whom ye also are builded together** for an habitation of God through the Spirit.

It's hard to fathom that the God who created the universe would want His home to be inside of our bodies. However, if you've been born again that is exactly the case.

> 1 Corinthians 3:16 Know ye not that **ye are the temple of God, and that the Spirit of God dwelleth in you**?

Once you come to Christ and have been born again, you've lost ownership of your body and spirit. They now belong to God. He paid the price for you. He owns you! You're no longer the captain of the ship. The price He paid was the blood of Jesus and He fully intends to keep what He paid for!

> 1 Corinthians 6:19 What? know ye not that **your body is the temple** of the Holy Ghost which is in you, which ye have of God, and **ye are not your own?**
> 1 Corinthians 6:20 For **ye are bought with a price**: therefore glorify God in your body, and in your spirit, **which are God's**.

When you trust in Jesus and are Born Again, you become part of God's Temple. Furthermore, you enter into an Everlasting Covenant with God. What does it mean to be in an Everlasting Covenant and how long is Everlasting? Everlasting means it will never end!

| 2 Corinthians 6:16 And what agreement hath the temple of God with idols? for **ye are the temple of the living God**; as God hath said, I will dwell in them, and walk in them; and **I will be their God, and they shall be my people**. | Jeremiah 32:38 And **they shall be my people, and I will be their God:**
Jeremiah 32:40 And **I will make an everlasting covenant with them**, that I will not turn away from them, to do them good; but I will put my fear in their hearts, that **they shall not depart from me.** |

God puts His fear in the heart of His true believers which ensures they will never depart from Him. This isn't the believer hanging on to Him. This is Him hanging on to the believer! We're going to explore this more and learn more about the Everlasting Covenant. This is the Covenant of Jesus the Son of David and of Abraham!

| Matthew 1:1 The book of the generation of **Jesus Christ, the son of David**, the son of Abraham. |

Children of the Lord

Jesus is the Son of David who was promised to come from David's lineage. Jesus had no physical children, but did you know that the Bible says that Christ would have spiritual children? We use different nouns when we refer to people depending on the context of the conversation and the nature of the relationship. For instance, you may be a father, a brother, a cousin, a son, etc depending on the context. You can be all these things at the same time, and you're not limited to one. It depends on the context of the relationship that's being referred to. It's the same way with Jesus and with our relationship to Him. In one way, we are brothers and sisters to Jesus and He is our Elder Brother. The Bible describes our relationship in that way. In another way, the Bible describes Jesus as our Husband, and believers are espoused to Christ. Jesus is God in flesh and so in another way, we are His creation. In another way, we are Children of Jesus, Children of Christ.

The Prophets said that Christ would be given children. They said that the time that He would receive His children would be when He died for their sins!

> Isaiah 53:10 Yet it pleased the LORD to bruise him; he hath put him to grief: <u>when thou shalt make his soul an offering for sin</u>, **he shall see his seed**, he shall prolong his days, and the pleasure of the LORD shall prosper in his hand.

David also prophesied of the Seed of Christ in Psalm 22. Psalm 22 talks about the crucifixion of Christ (1000 years before it happened) and at the end of Psalm 22 we learn that as a result of Christ's crucifixion, He will have a Seed that serves Him.

> Psalm 22:30 **A seed shall serve him**; <u>it shall be accounted to the Lord for a generation.</u>

God recognizes the Seed of Christ as one Generation. The Seed of Christ are Born Again Believers whom God calls a Chosen Generation and a Holy Nation!

> 1 Peter 2:9 But **ye are a chosen generation**, a royal priesthood, **an holy nation**, a peculiar people; that ye should shew forth the praises of him who hath called you out of darkness into his marvellous light;

Isaiah told us that the Children of Christ would do miracles in the land of Israel. He also said that the disciples of Christ would be given a law and testimony. The law Isaiah refers to is the New Testament Law to believe on Jesus and to love each other.

Isaiah 8:16 Bind up the testimony, <u>seal the law among my disciples.</u>	1 John 3:23 And this is his commandment, That we should <u>believe on the name of his Son Jesus Christ, and love one another,</u> as he gave us commandment. John 13:34 A new commandment I give unto you, <u>That ye love one another;</u> as I have loved you, that ye also love one another.
Isaiah 8:18 Behold, **I and the children whom the LORD hath given me** <u>are for signs and for wonders in Israel</u> from the LORD of hosts, which dwelleth in mount Zion.	(The writer of Hebrews refers to these verses) Hebrews 2:13 And again, <u>I will put my trust in him.</u> And again, **Behold I and the children which God hath given me.**
Isaiah 8:20 To the law and to the testimony: <u>if they speak not according to this word, it is because there is no light in them.</u> (Those who deny the Gospel have no light, in other words, no understanding and no life. When we trust in Jesus we are given understanding and life!) (Those who have the light are Children of Light-Children of the Lord!)	John 8:12 Then spake Jesus again unto them, saying, **I am the light of the world**: he that followeth me shall not walk in darkness, <u>but shall have the light of life.</u> John 12:36 While ye have light, <u>believe in the light,</u> **that ye may be the children of light.** These things spake Jesus, and departed, and did hide himself from them.

Isaiah shows us something special about the Seed of Christ regarding the Holy Spirit. In the Old Testament, God would send His Spirit upon men at times. It was by His Spirit that the Prophets prophesied and wrote scripture. It was also by God's Spirit that certain men such as Elijah and Elisha were able to perform miracles. The Holy Spirit was upon them, but it wasn't always permanent. He remained upon them until they accomplished the task that God wanted them to accomplish. They didn't have the indwelling of the Holy Spirit that Born Again Believers have. It's important to understand the difference between the Holy Spirit coming upon a person and the Holy Spirit dwelling within a person because in the Old Testament, you'll see the Spirit come upon men such as King Saul and then you'll see the Spirit leave that person.

God had revealed to John the Baptist that Christ would have the Spirit come upon Him, and this would be something John would see. When the Holy Spirit came upon Christ it would remain on Him. John saw the Holy Spirit come upon Jesus when Jesus came to be baptized.

John 1:33 And I knew him not: but he that sent me to baptize with water, the same said unto me, **Upon whom thou shalt see the Spirit descending, and remaining on him**, the same is he which baptizeth with the Holy Ghost.

Now, here's the special thing about the Seed of Christ regarding the Spirit. God made a covenant with Christ and His Seed. God says that the Spirit that is upon Christ will not leave Him. The Spirit that is upon Him will not leave nor the words in His mouth, in other words, His Testimony. But it's not just Christ, the Spirit that is upon the Seed of Christ will not leave them either! The words of their mouth will not leave either, so they won't testify that they've been saved by Jesus and then change their Testimony!

> Isaiah 59:21 As for me, **this is my covenant with them**, saith the LORD; **My spirit that is upon thee, and my words which I have put in thy mouth, <u>shall not depart out of thy mouth, nor out of the mouth of thy seed, nor out of the mouth of thy seed's seed</u>**, saith the LORD, from henceforth and for ever.

If you've been Born Again, God has made a Covenant with you that the Holy Spirit will never leave you! This contrasts with what some Christians teach. However, God gives many Covenant Promises to the Believer throughout His word that proves this!

As Believers, we are not only the Seed of Christ, but we also have a Spiritual Mother. In the Bible, the citizens of a city were referred to as that city's children. Cities are always referred to as women in the Bible, never men. An example of this is in Ezekial where God is speaking to the citizens of Jerusalem and comparing them with the citizens of Sodom. Prophetically, Sodom is Jerusalem's sister, and the daughters of Sodom are the citizens of Sodom.

> Ezekiel 16:48 As I live, saith the Lord GOD, **Sodom thy sister** hath not done, **she nor her daughters**, as thou hast done, **thou and thy daughters.**

God often speaks to cities in the Bible. However, when He speaks to a city He is never speaking to the houses and streets. He is never speaking to inanimate material. Anytime God speaks to a city in the Bible He is always speaking to its citizens. Jesus once pronounced judgment on Chorazin and Bethsaida which were two cities He had visited and performed miracles in. When He spoke to these cities He was speaking to their citizens.

> Matthew 11:21 **Woe unto thee, Chorazin! woe unto thee, Bethsaida**! for if the mighty works, which were done in you, had been done in Tyre and Sidon, they would have repented long ago in sackcloth and ashes.

Likewise, He spoke to Jerusalem in the same manner referring to their unbelief. Again, He is speaking to the citizens of Jerusalem.

> Matthew 23:37 **O Jerusalem, Jerusalem**, thou that killest the prophets, and stonest them which are sent unto thee, how often would I have gathered thy children together, even as a hen gathereth her chickens under her wings, and ye would not!

The reason it's important for you to understand how God speaks to cities and their citizens is because as Believers we are also citizens of a city. However, our city is not on the earth right now. It will be one day. Our city is Heavenly Jerusalem. When a person is Born Again, they become a citizen of New Jerusalem!

Hebrews 12:22 But ye are come unto mount Sion, and unto **the city of the living God, the heavenly Jerusalem**, and to an innumerable company of angels,

---

It's a great thing to be a citizen of New Jerusalem but there's a little more to it than that. Do you remember that I said we have a Spiritual Mother? Our mother is New Jerusalem. It's important to understand that New Jerusalem is different than the physical Jerusalem on earth now. God speaks to Physical Jerusalem and He speaks to New Jerusalem much in the Bible. If you want to understand these verses, you must distinguish as to which one He is referring to. Physical Jerusalem that is on the earth now represents the Old Covenant while New Jerusalem represents the New Covenant in scripture.

Galatians 4:24 Which things are an allegory: **for these are the two covenants;** the one from the mount Sinai, which gendereth to bondage, which is Agar.

Galatians 4:25 For this Agar is mount Sinai in Arabia, and answereth to **Jerusalem which now is, and is in bondage with her children**.

Physical Jerusalem is in bondage to sin because most of her citizens rejected Jesus Christ. However, the citizens of New Jerusalem are free because we have trusted in Jesus and He has freed us!

> Galatians 4:26 But Jerusalem which is above is free, **which is the mother of us all.**

Christ is a Spiritual Father to the Believer and New Jerusalem is our Spiritual Mother. New Jerusalem is also the Bride of Christ. New Jerusalem represents the entire Body of Christ. Just as a man and woman become one when they are married, Jesus will become one with His Bride, the Body of Christ one day!

> Revelation 21:9 And there came unto me one of the seven angels which had the seven vials full of the seven last plagues, and talked with me, saying, Come hither, **I will shew thee the bride, the Lamb's wife.**
>
> Revelation 21:10 And he carried me away in the spirit to a great and high mountain, and shewed me **that great city, the holy Jerusalem, descending out of heaven** from God,

When that happens, New Jerusalem will take the name of Christ in the same way a woman takes a man's last name in our culture.

Jeremiah 23:6 In his days Judah shall be saved, and Israel shall dwell safely: and this is his name whereby **he shall be called, THE LORD OUR RIGHTEOUSNESS.**	Jeremiah 33:16 In those days shall Judah be saved, and **Jerusalem** shall dwell safely: and this is the name wherewith **she** shall be called, **The LORD our righteousness.**

The prophets spoke of the glory and the blessings that New Jerusalem would receive in the Old Testament. The people anxiously awaited these promises. God told them not to despair because in due time New Jerusalem would start to have children. New Jerusalem didn't have any children until after Jesus died on the cross and the New Covenant was established. Yet, God promised New Jerusalem that she would bear children one day.

> Isaiah 54:1 Sing, **O barren, thou that didst not bear**; break forth into singing, and cry aloud, thou that didst not travail with child: **for more are the children of the desolate than the children of the married wife,** saith the LORD.

Not only would New Jerusalem have children, but she would have more children than the married wife which refers to the Old Covenant and physical Jerusalem.

> Galatians 4:27 For it is written, Rejoice, thou barren that bearest not; break forth and cry, thou that travailest not: for **the desolate hath many more children than she which hath an husband.**

At the time that Isaiah wrote about New Jerusalem, she wasn't married because the New Covenant had not been established. The New Covenant was not in full force and established until after Jesus died.

> Hebrews 9:16 For where a testament is, there must also of necessity be the death of the testator.

When Jesus died, New Jerusalem started having children! God said that New Jerusalem was going to suffer the loss of the children that was supposed to have been hers, referring to most of the Jews who should have accepted Jesus but didn't. However, He said she would have other children and that there would be so many that the physical land couldn't contain them!

> Isaiah 49:20 **The children which thou shalt have, after thou hast lost the other**, shall say again in thine ears, <u>The place is too strait for me: give place to me that I may dwell.</u>

Then, New Jerusalem sees her children (prophetically speaking) and she doesn't recognize them because they don't look like Hebrews. She asks God who these people are.

> Isaiah 49:21 Then shalt **thou say in thine heart, Who hath begotten me these**, seeing I have lost my children, and am desolate, a captive, and removing to and fro? and who hath brought up these? Behold, I was left alone; **these, where had they been?**

God replies to New Jerusalem and tells her that these children that she doesn't recognize are Gentiles and that He is going to visit the Gentiles and cause them to become sons and daughters of New Jerusalem!

> Isaiah 49:22 Thus saith the Lord GOD, Behold, **I will lift up mine hand to the Gentiles**, and set up my standard to the people: and **they shall bring thy sons in their arms, and thy daughters** shall be carried upon their shoulders.

God always wanted the Gentiles to be included in His Salvation. God speaking as Christ in Isaiah, says that it will seem at first like Christ failed to gather His people. He shows that Jacob (physical Israel) will reject Him.

> Isaiah 49:5 And now, saith <u>the LORD that formed me from the womb to be his servant</u>, **to bring Jacob again to him, Though Israel be not gathered,** yet shall I be glorious in the eyes of the LORD, and my God shall be my strength.

However, He then reveals that the reason for this is because He wanted to offer salvation to the Gentiles!

> Isaiah 49:6 And he said, <u>It is a light thing that thou shouldest be my servant to raise up the tribes of Jacob, and to restore the preserved of Israel:</u> **I will also give thee for a light to the Gentiles**, that thou mayest be my salvation unto the end of the earth.

If the Jews accepted Jesus immediately, the Kingdom of Heaven would have begun and there would be no such thing as what we call the Church Age. Today we are in what many refer to as the "Church Age" which is a time frame where God is putting together the Body of Christ which is made up of Jews and Gentiles. So, God made sure that the political and religious rulers in Israel would be people who were blind to who He was. This would keep most of the Jews from also realizing who Jesus is.

> Isaiah 29:10 For the LORD hath poured out upon you the spirit of deep sleep, and **hath closed your eyes: the prophets and your rulers, the seers hath he covered.**

So, even though there are many Jews who do believe in Jesus, most of them don't yet. God is allowing this to happen so that He can have mercy on as many people as possible.

Romans 11:32 For God hath concluded them all in unbelief, that he might have mercy upon all.

When God speaks to New Jerusalem, He is speaking to her citizens. That's one of the things I established earlier. That's important because He gives many promises to New Jerusalem. God tells New Jerusalem that Christ is her Husband again in Isaiah.

Isaiah 54:5 For **thy Maker is thine husband;** the LORD of hosts is his name; and thy Redeemer the Holy One of Israel; **The God of the whole earth shall he be called.**	Jesus is the Lord of Host, the Redeemer, and the Holy One of Israel. God says here that Jesus will be called the God of the whole earth!

God goes on to tell the citizens of New Jerusalem (Born Again Christians), that He will show them Everlasting Mercy!

Isaiah 54:8 In a little wrath I hid my face from thee for a moment; but **with everlasting kindness will I have mercy on thee**, saith the LORD thy Redeemer.

God swears that He will never again be wroth with us which means extremely angry, and He will never rebuke us which means to strongly disapprove of!

Isaiah 54:9 For this is as the waters of Noah unto me: for as I have sworn that the waters of Noah should no more go over the earth; **so have I sworn that I would not be wroth with thee, nor rebuke thee.**

God also says that His kindness will NEVER depart from us. His Covenant that He establishes with us will NOT BE REMOVED!

Isaiah 54:10 For the mountains shall depart, and the hills be removed; but **my kindness shall not depart from thee, neither shall the covenant of my peace be removed**, saith the LORD that hath mercy on thee.

God tells New Jerusalem that all her children will be taught by the Lord and that they will have a great deal of peace!

Isaiah 54:13 And **all thy children shall be taught of the LORD**; and great shall be the peace of thy children.

Jesus tells us about the children who are taught by God. If you read the entire chapter (John 6) you will see that the children taught by God are those who come to Him and believe in Him. Those who profess faith but then leave were never taught by God (Jesus says this in John 6).

> John 6:45 <u>It is written in the prophets</u>, And **they shall be all taught of God**. Every man therefore that hath heard, and hath learned of the Father, cometh unto me

Isaiah 54:13 And **all thy children shall be taught of the LORD**; and great shall be the peace of thy children.	Jeremiah 31:34 And **they shall teach** no more every man his neighbour, and every man his brother, saying, Know the LORD: **for they shall all know me, from the least of them unto the greatest of them**, saith the LORD: for I will forgive their iniquity, and I will remember their sin no more.

All the citizens of New Jerusalem have been taught by God. Also, all the citizens of New Jerusalem KNOW THE LORD. Every Born-Again person "Knows the Lord". There will be people who go to church all their lives and who do good works who were never Born Again. There will be very religious people who think they are going to Heaven who will never see it because they never totally put their trust in Jesus. They believed in Jesus in their minds, but it never sank into their heart, and they trusted that their good works contributed to their salvation. God will tell these people He never knew them because they were never Born Again. However, He will not tell anyone who has been Born Again that He never knew them because the Bible plainly tells us that ALL BORN AGAIN CHRISTIANS KNOW THE LORD!

When we put our Trust in Jesus, we become Children of the Lord. Only sinless people can be Children of the Lord; however, God gives the Seed of Christ His righteousness so that we are sinless in His eyes (not that we are sinless, but Jesus is!).

Galatians 3:26 For ye are all the children of God by faith in Christ Jesus.

One day the Children of the Lord will go to our City and God will give us comfort there!

Isaiah 66:13 **As one whom his mother comforteth**, so will I comfort you; and **ye shall be comforted in Jerusalem**.

The Fountain of Living Waters

Water is essential to life. They say that our bodies are 50-75 percent water. Every part of our bodies functions better when we have plenty of water. You can't survive too long without any water. If you're ever planning a trip or activity where you're going to be outdoors or away from civilization for a good amount of time, the first thing you need to make sure you have is water. It's more important than food.

If you ever find yourself outdoors or needing water for any reason and you don't have your own water, you need to look for running water. Water that is moving is cleaner because if anything unclean falls into it, it can purify itself and push anything foul downstream. Water that isn't moving, like a puddle or pond, will collect impurities and get dirtier over time as animals use it or something unclean gets into it.

The Bible calls moving water Living Water. God often compares Himself to water in the Bible, because just as natural water sustains us and gives us life, He is the ultimate source of our life. Not only does water nourish the body but it also cleanses.

In Leviticus, God gives Israel instructions about what to do when they come into contact with unclean things. For instance, if an unclean animal such as a mouse died in your bed, your bed would be unclean. You would then have to wash it before you could use it again or else you and the bed would be unclean. If the mouse fell in a bucket of water, the water would be unclean, and you'd have to pour it out. However, if the mouse fell into a large pool of water that was fed by a spring, it would remain clean because the pool of water would be able to purify itself.

Leviticus 11:36 Nevertheless **a fountain or pit, wherein there is plenty of water, shall be clean:** but that which toucheth their carcase shall be unclean.

Now, God is our source of life. He sustains us and He purifies us. He is the ultimate Fountain of Living Waters, for it is from Him that we have life. Our hearts beat because He makes them beat, and we breathe because He gives us air.

Psalm 36:8 They shall be abundantly satisfied with the fatness of thy house; and **thou shalt make them drink of the river of thy pleasures**.

Psalm 36:9 **For with thee is the fountain of life**: in thy light shall we see light.

In the days of Jeremiah, most of Israel had forsaken the Lord. There were different groups of people in Israel at the time of Jeremiah. There was a small group of people who still trusted in the Lord, but most of the people had forsaken Him, in other words, abandoned Him.

> Jeremiah 17:13 O LORD, the hope of Israel, all that forsake thee shall be ashamed, and they that depart from me shall be written in the earth, because **they have forsaken the LORD, the fountain of living waters.**

Not only did they forsake the Lord by ceasing to Trust in Him, but they had substituted their Trust in Him for other gods and/or their own righteousness.

> Jeremiah 2:13 For my people have committed two evils; **they have forsaken me the fountain of living waters,** and hewed them out cisterns, broken cisterns, that can hold no water.

God had shown Israel that He was their Fountain of Living Waters when they came out of Egypt. Remember Moses and the Rock in the wilderness? Water came out of a Rock in the desert and nourished millions of people. In Psalm 114, we learn the Rock was a flint rock.

> Psalm 114:8 Which turned the rock into a standing water, **the flint into a fountain of waters.**

Paul tells us that the Rock represents Jesus!

> 1 Corinthians 10:4 And did all drink the same spiritual drink: for they drank of that spiritual Rock that followed them: **and that Rock was Christ.**

Jesus once met a woman at a well in Samaria. He asked the woman if she'd draw Him some water out of the well, which she thought was weird because He was a Jew and Jews and Samaritans didn't get along. As she is contemplating and hesitating, Jesus tells the woman that He had Living Water that He would give her and that she'd ask Him for this water if she knew who He was!

> John 4:10 Jesus answered and said unto her, If thou knewest the gift of God, and who it is that saith to thee, Give me to drink; **thou wouldest have asked of him, and he would have given thee living water.**

The woman then proceeds to ask Jesus how and where He would get this Living Water since he didn't have a bucket or anything to get water with from the well.

> John 4:11 The woman saith unto him, <u>Sir, thou hast nothing to draw with,</u> and the well is deep: **from whence then hast thou that living water?**

Jesus tells the woman that His water doesn't come from the well. He tells her the well water would only provide temporary sustainment.

> John 4:13 Jesus answered and said unto her, **Whosoever drinketh of this water shall thirst again:**

However, Jesus tells the woman that His water would provide Eternal Life! Whoever drinks the water that Jesus gives will NEVER thirst again! Not only that, but the water He gives will remain in that person and will become a well that is spring fed, and it will last ETERNALLY!

> John 4:14 But **whosoever drinketh of the water that I shall give him shall <u>never</u> thirst**; but the water that I shall give him shall be in him **a well of water springing up into everlasting life**.

When you Trust in Jesus and are Born Again, God has promised you will never hunger or thirst again. If you were Born Again but were somehow able to lose your salvation these verses wouldn't be true. If you truly drank of the water Jesus gives, but then later thirsted, God's word wouldn't be accurate.

John 6:35 And Jesus said unto them, I am the bread of life: he that cometh to me **shall <u>never</u> hunger**; and he that believeth on me **shall <u>never</u> thirst**.	Isaiah 49:10 **They shall not hunger nor thirst**; neither shall the heat nor sun smite them: for he that hath mercy on them shall lead them, **even by the springs of water shall he guide them.**

The opponent of this doctrine would tell you that you must keep drinking. In other words, it's not just one drink, but you keep yourself in good graces with God by your good works. However, that's the opposite of what Jesus teaches. We don't keep drinking by our good works, we keep drinking because of the Fountain of Living Water that Jesus puts in our spirit!

You see, Jesus tells us that this Water is the Holy Spirit that will be inside of the Believer! In Isaiah, we are shown that these waters will not fail, in other words, the water doesn't stop flowing!

Isaiah 58:11 And the LORD shall guide thee continually, and satisfy thy soul in drought, and make fat thy bones: **and thou shalt be like a watered garden, and like a spring of water, whose waters fail not.**

Jesus offers His water to anyone who is thirsty.

John 7:37 In the last day, that great day of the feast, Jesus stood and cried, saying, **If any man thirst, let him come unto me, and drink**.

Jesus then refers to Isaiah and the water that will flow out of the person who puts their Trust in Him.

John 7:38 **He that believeth on me**, as the scripture hath said, **out of his belly shall flow rivers of living water.**

The Apostle John who penned this quote, then tells us that Jesus was referring to the Holy Spirit. This means the Holy Spirit inside of the Believer is the Eternal Spring of Water. However, this was not available until after Jesus rose from the dead. This is only available to Born Again Believers.

John 7:39 (**But this spake he of the Spirit**, **which they that believe on him should receive**: for the Holy Ghost was not yet given; because that Jesus was not yet glorified.)

Now, we remember that in addition to water giving us life and drink, it also cleanses us. We as sinners, require cleansing and the Lord must wash us. The Lord promises His people that He will cleanse them from their sins if they Trust in Him.

Isaiah 1:18 Come now, and let us reason together, saith the LORD: **though your sins be as scarlet, they shall be as white as snow**; though they be red like crimson, they shall be as wool.

The Lord promises He will wash our sins away so that our souls are as white as snow.

Psalm 51:2 **Wash me** throughly from mine iniquity, and cleanse me from my sin.
Psalm 51:7 Purge me with hyssop, and I shall be clean: **wash me, and I shall be whiter than snow.**

Only the Lord can wash us. Job knew that he couldn't make himself clean in God's eyes. You can't get clean through religion. It won't work. You'll never be clean enough. Anyone who tries to come to God by cleaning up their life in the power of their flesh will be plunged into a ditch (thrown into hell).

Job 9:30 **If I wash myself with snow water**, and make my hands never so clean;

Job 9:31 **Yet shalt thou plunge me in the ditch**, and mine own clothes shall abhor me.

To be in God's presence we must be washed with pure water. Jesus is the only One who can wash our sins away. The prophets told of this cleansing that God would provide, and the New Testament shows us that it would come through faith in Jesus.

Hebrews 10:22 Let us draw near with a true heart in full assurance of faith, having our hearts sprinkled from an evil conscience, **and our bodies washed with pure water.**	Ezekiel 36:25 **Then will I sprinkle clean water upon you, and ye shall be clean**: from all your filthiness, and from all your idols, will I cleanse you.

Not long before Jesus went to the cross, He washed His disciples' feet. When He did this, He established a few important principles. First, to be in a relationship with Him, He must wash you (cleanse you from your sins).

John 13:8 Peter saith unto him, Thou shalt never wash my feet. Jesus answered him, **If I wash thee not, thou hast no part with me.**

Second, when Jesus washes you, you are completely clean. You do not need to wash yourself at this point because He says He has totally and completely cleansed you!

John 13:10 Jesus saith to him, **He that is washed** needeth not save **to** wash his feet**, but is clean every whit:** and ye are clean, but not all.

Lastly, Jesus establishes the principle of feet washing. When we walk in the world our feet get dirty both literally and figuratively. Jesus told His disciples to wash each other's feet. This isn't just about keeping our feet clean literally, but more so about keeping each other accountable and clean from the moral pollutions of the world.

John 13:10 Jesus saith to him, He that is washed **needeth not save to wash his feet,** but is clean every whit: and ye are clean, but not all.

John 13:14 If I then, your Lord and Master, have washed your feet; **ye also ought to wash one another's feet.**

Remember, this has nothing to do with keeping us saved. Jesus already provided the complete cleansing. He completely cleansed our spirit. We hold each other accountable as Christians for the sake of the Church and to help each other walk through this sinful world.

Jesus is the Fountain of Living Waters. He is the source, the Fountain from which the Living Water flows. The Living Water that comes from Him is the Holy Spirit which becomes an Eternal Spring or Eternal source of Life within the Believer. Remember, we learned in Leviticus that if a mouse were to fall in a well of water that was fed by a spring, it would remain clean? The spring or fountain would cleanse the body of water and flush out the impurities. That's what the Holy Spirit does inside of the Believer. The Holy Spirit inside of the Believer is like a spring of water. The Bible says the Holy Spirit renews the Believer. To renew something is to restore it and to make it like new.

| Titus 3:5 Not by works of righteousness which we have done, but according to his mercy he saved us, **by the <u>washing</u> of regeneration, and <u>renewing</u> of the Holy Ghost;** | The washing of regeneration is our spirit being regenerated or brought back to life by the Holy Spirit.

The renewing of the Holy Ghost is what the Holy Spirit/Ghost does inside of the Believer. Remember, He's the Spring of Water that flushes out the impurities and keeps us alive with a never-ending supply of water. |

Our physical bodies are in a state of decay. They are literally dying and wasting away. However, the Holy Spirit inside of the Believer renews the Spirit of the Believer every day! He is constantly restoring us spiritually! He flushes out the bad things that come in and gives us Living Water!

2 Corinthians 4:16 For which cause we faint not; but though our outward man perish, yet **the inward man is renewed day by day**.

One drink from the Fountain of Living Waters provides Eternal Life. A person drinks from the Fountain of Living Waters when they Trust in the Blood of Jesus and are Born Again. Eternal Life is Eternal… If we were saved but could lose our salvation, we could never have possessed "Eternal" life. At best, we could have been given life if that were the case. If you possess Eternal Life, it must continue Eternally or it was never Eternal Life.

Jesus said that those who believe in Him would NEVER die. Even though they died physically they would still be alive. That means our loved ones who have passed away but have Trusted in Jesus and were Born Again are still alive!

John 11:25 Jesus said unto her, I am the resurrection, and the life: **he that believeth in me, though he were dead, yet shall he live**:

Furthermore, those who have been Born Again and are still physically alive SHALL NEVER DIE!

John 11:26 And **whosoever liveth and believeth in me <u>shall never die</u>**. Believest thou this?

If someone was truly Born Again through Faith in Jesus but then lost their Salvation, then the statement Jesus made in John 11:26 would not be totally accurate. In that case, the person would have believed in Jesus but died in contrast to the statement that Jesus made. However, I will tell you that the statement is totally accurate and that Salvation is Forever and Eternal!

David's Mercies

Has anyone ever shown you Mercy? To be shown Mercy is to be spared some treatment or punishment that you had coming to you so to speak, or to be shown compassion or leniency when it was otherwise within someone's power to punish you. Mercy is not for innocent people but for the guilty. An example of Mercy is when a police officer is about to give you a speeding ticket but then decides to show you a little compassion and lets you off with a warning.

We talked about Living Water in the previous chapter. The Bible says this Water is available to anyone who is thirsty for it. The Bible also tells us that the Water is free. You don't need any money for the Water!

Isaiah 55:1 Ho, **every one that thirsteth, come ye to the waters, and he that hath no money**; come ye, buy, and eat; yea, come, buy wine and milk without money and without price.

God also tells us to listen to what He has to say. If we hear His message, it will cause our Souls to live! Furthermore, He says that He will make an Everlasting Covenant with us. This Covenant is not to a Nation, but rather it is to whomever is thirsty for it. The nature of the Covenant He offers to the individual is that it is Everlasting, which means it will last Eternally. Furthermore, the person with whom He makes the Covenant with shall receive the <u>Sure Mercies of David</u>.

> Isaiah 55:3 Incline your ear, and come unto me: <u>hear, and your soul shall live</u>; and **I will make an everlasting covenant with you, even the sure mercies of David.**

This Covenant is the New Covenant the Prophets spoke of, and Paul tells us this Covenant came into power when Jesus rose from the dead, which is also what we are told in other New Testament books regarding the New Covenant.

> Acts 13:34 And as concerning that he raised him up from the dead, now no more to return to corruption, **he said on this wise, I will give you the sure mercies of David.**

All Born Again Christians receive the Sure Mercies of David. If God has given us the Sure Mercies of David, we need to find out what this entails. First, let's define the word "Sure". We often use the term "sure thing" in our society but often when we say sure thing, it's not sure at all. The word "Sure" means to be certain, positively confident, to have no doubt, or to be inevitable. In other words, the Born Again Believer is positively certain to receive the Mercies of David.

David's Mercies are described in the Old Testament. Now, David was a top-notch guy. Please understand, as a man David was right up there with the best morally speaking. However, David wasn't perfect. The only Perfect Man that has walked the earth is Jesus. Even men who love the Lord and have a relationship with Him, are flawed in the flesh. Even men who love the Lord can sin grotesquely at times. They won't walk in those sins and live a lifestyle of disobedience to God, but they can and do have moral failures.

David had a moral failure at a point in his life and sinned against God. As a matter of fact, the sins that David committed during that period are the kind of sins that bring severe judgment and chastisement from God. God had previously taken the lives of men in the Old Testament for committing lesser sins than those that David committed during this time. David understood this and he cried out to God, begging for His Mercy.

Psalm 51:1 **Have mercy upon me, O God**, according to thy lovingkindness: according unto the multitude of thy tender mercies **blot out my transgressions**.

Psalm 51:11 Cast me not away from thy presence; and take not thy holy spirit from me.

God spoke to David through the Prophet Nathan and told David that his sin had been put away and that he would not die. However, God did punish David for his sins and David suffered greatly. Nonetheless, God forgave David and remained in relationship with him.

> 2 Samuel 12:13 And David said unto Nathan, I have sinned against the LORD. And Nathan said unto David, **The LORD also hath put away thy sin; thou shalt not die.**

When God told David that He put away his sin, David understood that God was providing an atonement for him. David also understood that while he was guilty, God was not imputing his sins to his account. The atonement that God provided for David was the blood of Jesus, and He applied Jesus's blood to David as payment for David's sins. David's response to God's Mercy was gratitude and a realization that he was Blessed.

> Psalm 32:1 **Blessed** is he whose transgression is forgiven, **whose sin is covered**.
> Psalm 32:2 **Blessed** is the man unto whom the LORD **imputeth not iniquity**, and in whose spirit there is no guile.

The Apostle Paul tells us that the Born-Again Believer is Blessed in the same manner as David.

> Romans 4:6 Even as David also describeth **the blessedness of the man, unto whom God imputeth righteousness without works,**
> Romans 4:7 Saying, Blessed are they whose iniquities are forgiven, and whose sins are covered.
> Romans 4:8 **Blessed is the man to whom the Lord <u>will not</u> impute sin**.

You see, he doesn't say Blessed is the man who does not sin. As long as we're in the flesh, we all have some magnitude of sin. The issue for the Believer is that the Lord is not imputing sin to the Believer's account.

It was a great blessing to David when God showed him Mercy, after his moral failure. However, this wasn't the only Mercy that God showed to David. In fact, there were other mercies given to David that were even more of a blessing to him, and David sings about these mercies in Psalm 89.

Psalm 89:1 **I will sing of the mercies of the LORD** for ever: with my mouth will I make known thy faithfulness to all generations.

Psalm 89:2 For I have said, **Mercy shall be built up for ever**: thy faithfulness shalt thou establish in the very heavens.

The reason these mercies are so important to David is because they extend to his seed which is his Son. God made a covenant with David regarding a Son that he was going to have with whom God would give an Everlasting Kingdom to.

Psalm 89:3 **I have made a covenant with my chosen**, I have sworn unto David my servant,
Psalm 89:4 Thy seed will I establish for ever, and build up thy throne to all generations. Selah.

At this point, we need to understand something about how the Bible refers to the Messiah, which we know is Jesus. In the Old Testament, the Messiah is sometimes called David because he is the Son of David. When the Old Testament prophets referred to the Son of David or the "Greater David", He would simply be called David. Understand, these were written hundreds of years after David the son of Jesse had already died.

Jeremiah 30:9 But they shall serve the LORD their God, and **David their king, whom I will raise up unto them.**	Hosea 3:5 Afterward shall the children of Israel return, and seek the LORD their God, **and David their king**; and shall fear the LORD and his goodness in the latter days.	Ezekiel 37:24 **And David my servant shall be king over them;** and they all shall have one shepherd: they shall also walk in my judgments, and observe my statutes, and do them.

It's important to understand how the scriptures speak of the Messiah and call him David because, in Psalm 89, David writes about the Son of David and calls him David, although he is not referring to himself but the Messiah. David had a vision about God anointing the Messiah.

> Psalm 89:19 Then thou spakest in vision to thy holy one, and saidst, I have laid help upon one that is mighty; **I have exalted one chosen out of the people.**
> Psalm 89:20 I have found David my servant; with my holy oil have I anointed him:

We know God is speaking of Christ here because of the way He is described. Among other things, God says that He (Christ) will be God's Firstborn who is higher than the kings of the earth.

> Psalm 89:27 Also **I will make him my firstborn**, higher than the kings of the earth.

God then references the Covenant, which was originally spoken to David, however we see that God's Mercy is going to extend to the Seed of Christ!

Psalm 89:28 **My mercy will I keep for him for evermore**, and my covenant shall stand fast with him.

Psalm 89:29 **His seed also will I make to endure for ever**, and his throne as the days of heaven.

Why would Christ need Mercy? Christ doesn't need Mercy for Himself because He is the Sinless and the Perfect Son of God. However, the Seed of Christ does need Mercy and we will see how God's Mercy extends to Christ's Seed!

Psalm 89:30 **If his children forsake my law**, and walk not in my judgments;

Psalm 89:31 If they break my statutes, and **keep not my commandments;**

Psalm 89:32 **Then will I visit their transgression with the rod**, and their iniquity with stripes.

Psalm 89:33 **Nevertheless my lovingkindness will I not utterly take from him, nor suffer my faithfulness to fail.**

God says that when the Seed of Christ sins, He will chastise them. However, He will not send them to Hell! God goes on to make a promise and establish the security of Christ's Seed.

> Psalm 89:34 **My covenant will I not break,** nor alter the thing that is gone out of my lips.
>
> Psalm 89:35 **Once have I sworn by my holiness** that I will not lie unto David.
>
> Psalm 89:36 **His seed shall endure for ever,** and his throne as the sun before me.
>
> Psalm 89:37 It shall be established for ever as the moon, and as a faithful witness in heaven. Selah.

GOD HAS MADE A COVENANT PROMISE THAT THE SEED OF CHRIST WILL ENDURE! HE HAS SWORN BY HIS HOLINESS! This section ends with verse 37 and the last word is "Selah" which means "think or meditate on this".

As flesh and blood people, it's hard for us to grasp the Mercy of God. You see, our Mercy is limited. The way most of us think is that we can take so much but eventually Mercy will run out. Some Christians think that God will show Mercy for a while but eventually, He is going to get fed up and His Mercy will expire. However, David understood that God's Mercy Endures Forever.

> Psalm 100:5 For the LORD is good; **his mercy is everlasting**; and his truth endureth to all generations.
>
> Psalm 118:1 O give thanks unto the LORD; for he is good: **because his mercy endureth for ever.**

Abraham is known as the Father of Faith and the model of those who would put their Trust in the Lord and who would be counted Righteous because of their Faith and Trust rather than their works. Those of us who Trust in Jesus are spiritual children of Abraham.

> Galatians 3:7 Know ye therefore that **they which are of faith, the same are the children of Abraham.**

David is a model of the New Testament Believer and of the Mercy that God extends to the Believer. Jesus Christ came in the flesh as the Son of David.

> Romans 1:3 Concerning his Son Jesus Christ our Lord, **which was made of the seed of David according to the flesh;**

When Jesus conquered life and death, He secured Everlasting Mercy for His children.

> Hebrews 2:13 And again, I will put my trust in him. And again, **Behold I and the children which God hath given me**.
> Hebrews 2:14 **Forasmuch then as the children are partakers of flesh and blood, he also himself likewise took part of the same**; that through death he might destroy him that had the power of death, that is, the devil;
> Hebrews 2:17 Wherefore in all things it behoved him to be made like unto his brethren, **that he might be a <u>merciful</u> and faithful high priest** in things pertaining to God, **to make reconciliation for the sins of the people.**

As the Seed of Christ, the Born-Again Believer is promised EVERLASTING MERCY!

Chastised Children

God has given His Children Everlasting Mercy. If we truly understood how much Mercy we have been given we would all live more holy than we do. Paul begs the Romans to live holy lives because of the Mercy that they've been shown, and he also tells them it's only reasonable that they do this service. In other words, due to the Mercy that they've been given, it only makes good sense for them to present their lives as a living sacrifice to God by living holy.

Romans 12:1 I beseech you therefore, brethren, **by the mercies of God**, that ye present your bodies a living sacrifice, holy, acceptable unto God, **which is your reasonable service**.

The problem that we have as Christians is that although our spirits are reborn, we are still in a body of flesh that is prone to sin. Our flesh isn't reborn and so our spirit and our flesh are at odds with each other. Because of this, we can't be perfect as long as we're in these bodies. Along with the voice of the Spirit, God the Father has promised to chastise His children when they sin.

Remember God's promise to David and to the Seed of Christ. When we sin, God has promised that our transgression is going to be visited with the rod.

> Psalm 89:31 If they break my statutes, and keep not my commandments;
> Psalm 89:32 **Then will I visit their transgression with the rod**, and their iniquity with stripes.

When God speaks of using the rod you may think that sounds harsh, especially today, but it's an act of love. In fact, God says that those who spare the rod for their children hate them. One of the reasons that society is in such a mess today is that children grow up without a healthy reverence and respect for anything. When children learn that there are going to be negative consequences for immoral behavior, they become better people and better citizens. The Bible doesn't advocate abuse or physically harming a child. What we're talking about is sensible discipline.

> Proverbs 13:24 He that spareth his rod hateth his son: but **he that loveth him chasteneth him betimes.**

God makes a division in His word between how He judges the world and how He judges His children. You see, normally parents only chastise their own kids. If you go around spanking other people's kids, then you're bound to run into trouble and eventually receive a spanking of your own. God only chastises His children, those who have been Born-Again and are Children of the Lord.

The rest of the world will be judged and punished accordingly someday. However, for now, God doesn't provide spiritual correction in their lives. If God never provides spiritual correction, then you're not His child.

Hebrews 12:7 **If ye endure chastening, God dealeth with you as with sons**; for what son is he whom the father chasteneth not?

Hebrews 12:8 **But if ye be without chastisement**, whereof all are partakers, **then are ye bastards, and not sons**.

It's never fun to receive a spanking or to receive correction from someone. However, sometimes you can look back and see how that correction was beneficial in your life. If God is chastising you, then you are Blessed! That means He cares about you, and He cares about what is going on in your life.

Psalm 94:12 **Blessed is the man whom thou chastenest**, O LORD, and teachest him out of thy law;

When you understand that God is taking action and correcting you, it should make you happy. Although it's painful in the moment, this is proof your Father in Heaven loves you and sees you!

Job 5:17 Behold, **happy is the man whom God correcteth**: therefore despise not thou the chastening of the Almighty:

We shouldn't get angry when the Lord disciplines us or grow weary as if it's some dreadful thing that is happening. God is teaching us to be more like Him.

Proverbs 3:11 My son, despise not the chastening of the LORD; neither be weary of his correction:

Proverbs 3:12 **For whom the LORD loveth he correcteth**; even as a father the son in whom he delighteth.

God chastises His children for their profit and so they might be more like Him. It's in our best interest to live like God wants. Sin brings nothing but pain. We may think it's fun at the time, however, sin will always cause destruction in your life. It will never make anything better for you. God doesn't chastise His kids because He wants to hurt them but to help them.

Hebrews 12:10 For they verily for a few days chastened us after their own pleasure; **but he for our profit, that we might be partakers of his holiness.**

Hebrews 12:11 Now no chastening for the present seemeth to be joyous, but grievous: nevertheless **afterward it yieldeth the peaceable fruit of righteousness unto them which are exercised thereby.**

We could avoid some pain and prevent some spiritual correction if we'd use a little more common sense at times and make proper judgments in our lives.

We need to learn from our mistakes. We also need to read our Bibles more so that we know more about what God desires for us. God says if we'd use better judgment at times, we could prevent Him from having to chastise us.

> 1 Corinthians 11:31 For if we would judge ourselves, we should not be judged.

However, on the same note, God wants us to know that when He does judge us for doing something wrong, He chastens us as children and doesn't judge us in the same manner that He judges the world.

> 1 Corinthians 11:32 But **when we are judged, we are chastened of the Lord**, <u>that we should not be condemned with the world</u>.

It's important for you to know that you can spare yourself some pain because at times God's chastisement can be very painful even though it is ultimately for our good. As a Christian, you will be tempted to walk after the lust of your flesh. All people reap what they sow in one manner or another. Just because God doesn't deal with a Born-Again person the same way He deals with other people doesn't mean there are no consequences.

> Galatians 6:7 Be not deceived; God is not mocked: for whatsoever a man soweth, that shall he also reap.

If you sow to your flesh as a Christian, you're going to have problems with your flesh, with your physical body. This is one of God's promises to His people. Sowing to your flesh means you're giving the flesh what it wants. We're not talking about taking care of your body. God wants us to do that. We're talking about giving in to the sinful desires of the flesh such as committing fornication, which is just one example. God says that when we do this, we're going to reap corruption in our flesh. This means we're going to have physical issues such as sickness and even death. However, to the Born-Again Christian, the judgment is confined to our flesh. Our spirits remain saved and Born-Again.

> Galatians 6:8 For **he that soweth to his flesh <u>shall of the flesh</u> reap corruption**; but he that soweth to the Spirit shall of the Spirit reap life everlasting.

God pronounced judgment on our sins at the cross. The Believer's flesh is still under condemnation, but our spirits and souls are free when we are in Jesus.

> Romans 8:3 For what the law could not do, in that it was weak through the flesh, **God sending his own Son** in the likeness of sinful flesh, and for sin, **condemned sin in the flesh**:

God's chastisement can be so severe at times, that the recipient dies physically. This type of severe chastisement is usually reserved for people who cause damage to the Body of Christ and mar the name of the Church.

God doesn't take any pleasure in cutting a Believer's life short, but we have to understand that could be necessary and worthwhile in the long run if we damage the Church's image. The world needs to see a Holy Church in order to realize we're different and to see Jesus in us.

In Corinth, some of the members of the Church were getting drunk when taking Communion. Some of them were being gluttonous and not thinking about others during this time. They didn't have their thoughts focused on Jesus but were just enjoying the meal and thinking about themselves and their pleasure. As a result of this, God chastised them and some of them died physically. Understand, they were true Believers, and that's why God chastised them. Also understand, they didn't lose their Salvation! Paul says they slept, which is a New Testament term used several times to describe a Christian who has died physically and refers to their physical body. It never refers to a lost person.

> 1 Corinthians 11:30 **For this cause** many are weak and sickly among you, **and many sleep**.

Another example of severe chastisement is found in Corinthians. There was a man in the Church who was having a sexual relationship with his stepmother. Paul told the Church they needed to deliver him to Satan, which is a fancy way of saying they needed to kick him out of the Church and back into the world "Satan's Kingdom". You see, the man was marring the name and image of the Church, which could prevent others from becoming Christians. Also, the things he was doing were evidence that he might not have been truly Born-Again.

So, Paul says to kick him out of the church for the destruction of his flesh. If he was truly saved and continued in his sin, Paul was confident that the man's flesh would be destroyed. If he wasn't truly saved, this action may be what it took to give the man a reality check and make him examine his heart and "work out his salvation", which in turn could result in his salvation. That's why Paul says, "so that his spirit may be saved".

> 1 Corinthians 5:5 To deliver such an one unto Satan **for the destruction of the flesh, that the spirit may be saved** in the day of the Lord Jesus.

Most churches don't exorcise this type of discipline today which is why there's a lot of ungodliness in many churches. The Apostle Paul taught his churches to exercise church discipline and to not have fellowship with someone who claimed to be a Christian but was living immorally.

You may have heard the term "license to sin" used by someone who rejects Eternal Security. The idea is that if we are Eternally secure once we've been Born Again, we'd have a "license" to sin all we want as if there would be no consequence to our sin. This is a statement of ignorance to God's Word. Anyone who has read their Bible should know why this is an ignorant statement because the Bible is full of examples showing us the consequences people who were in a relationship with God faced when they sinned. Even though these people didn't lose their Salvation "because they were saved by grace through faith", they suffered greatly because of their sin.

When Israel left Egypt and approached the Promised Land, they feared entering the land and didn't trust the Lord the way they should have. This angered the Lord and He expressed His anger to Moses. Moses begged God to forgive the people and the Lord did.

> Numbers 14:19 **Pardon, I beseech thee**, the iniquity of this people **according unto the greatness of thy mercy**, and as thou hast forgiven this people, from Egypt even until now.
> Numbers 14:20 **And the LORD said, I have pardoned** according to thy word:

However, even though God forgave their sin, that didn't mean there weren't any consequences for their actions. God pardoned their sin. Nevertheless, He also chastised them, and as a consequence for their sin, all the people over 20 years old (with exception of Joshua and Caleb) died in the wilderness and never entered the Promised Land. Their children and the younger people were the ones who entered the land.

> Numbers 14:29 **Your carcases shall fall in this wilderness**; and all that were numbered of you, according to your whole number, from twenty years old and upward which have murmured against me.

When David sinned, God forgave David. However, like Israel, David suffered greatly because of his sin. Remember, when we damage the image of the church God is likely to chasten us severely. David damaged the image of Israel with his sin and one judgment was that David's child died.

> 2 Samuel 12:14 Howbeit, because **by this deed thou hast given great occasion to the enemies of the LORD to blaspheme**, the child also that is born unto thee shall surely die.

This wasn't the only judgment and chastening that David received. As a result of David's sin, he had family trouble for the rest of his life. David's sin caused a chain reaction and two more of David's sons died. One of David's sons murdered his other son and then that son was killed because of vengeance. David's sons were responsible for their actions. However, had David not sinned he would have held a higher reputation with them, and they may have confided in him and not have done what they did. David wept severely when his first son died.

> 2 Samuel 13:36 And it came to pass, as soon as he had made an end of speaking, that, behold, the king's sons came, and lifted up their voice and wept: and **the king also and all his servants wept very sore**.

When Absalom the second son died, David was completely broken.

> 2 Samuel 18:33 And the king was much moved, and went up to the chamber over the gate, and wept: and as he went, thus he said, **O my son Absalom, my son, my son Absalom! would God I had died for thee, O Absalom, my son, my son!**

After David sinned, God told him the sword would never depart his house, which referred to the family problems he was going to suffer.

> 2 Samuel 12:10 **Now therefore the sword shall never depart from thine house**; because thou hast despised me, and hast taken the wife of Uriah the Hittite to be thy wife.

Do you think that David felt like he got away with his sin? Do you think that since God showed David mercy and forgave him, David felt like there weren't any consequences? Do you think David felt like he had a license to sin? Our sin doesn't just affect ourselves. It hurts other people, and it may be the difference in whether someone gets saved. If you damage your reputation with a person, you could lose your influence and no longer be able to be a witness in that person's life. This could be the difference in whether or not someone turns to Jesus.

Sometimes God must chasten His people severely. He does this because He loves us. He also does this because He wants other people to be saved through our influence. Ultimately, God is trying to save as many people as possible and when our actions get in the way of that, we will have problems. Nevertheless, though we are chastened severely, God will not deliver us over to death. We will not go to Hell if we've truly been Born Again.

Psalm 118:18 The LORD hath chastened me sore: **but he hath not given me over unto death.**

5 Crowns

To understand what the Bible says about Salvation, it's crucial you understand the difference between a Gift and a Reward. A Gift by definition, is something that someone freely or voluntarily gives you, which is not compensation. A Reward, on the other hand, is something that is given in return for something, in other words, it is compensation. The Bible clearly tells us that Salvation is a <u>Free Gift</u> from God. That means Salvation is in no way a means of God compensating us for our good actions.

Romans 5:16 And not as it was by one that sinned, so is the gift: for the judgment was by one to condemnation, but **the free gift** is of many offences unto justification.	Romans 6:23 For the wages of sin is death; but **the gift of God is eternal life** through Jesus Christ our Lord.	Ephesians 2:8 **For by grace are ye saved through faith;** and that not of yourselves: **it is the gift of God:**

Furthermore, the Bible tells us that the Gifts and the Calling of God are without repentance! That means that God doesn't give someone a Gift and then change His mind and take it back! God won't give someone the Free Gift of Eternal Life and then take it back from them if they have a moral failure.

Romans 11:29 For the gifts and calling of God are without repentance.

We are also told in 2 Corinthians that Salvation will not be repented of or turned from. The context in this verse is comparing worldly sorrow to Godly sorrow. There are things in the world that will make you sorry and everyone in the world experiences sorrow at times, such as when a loved one dies. However, there is another kind of sorrow that God sends to His people that He calls to Salvation. It's the kind of sorrow that makes you realize you are lost without God and that you are a sinner. This type of sorrow results in the sinner repenting towards God and putting their trust in Jesus. The result of this sorrow is Salvation that will not be repented of! This verse tells us that true Salvation will not be turned from!

2 Corinthians 7:10 For godly sorrow worketh repentance to salvation **not to be repented of**: but the sorrow of the world worketh death.

The Bible also has a lot to say about Rewards. In contrast to a Gift, a Reward is worked for, and God tells us we can lose some of our Rewards! If God offers us Rewards in addition to Salvation, that should motivate us to work for them. There are some Rewards that will not be lost. For instance, Jesus says when we give a fellow believer a cup of water in His name, which means we are doing it for Him and we let the person know that, we will not lose our Reward.

Mark 9:41 For whosoever shall give you a cup of water to drink in my name, because ye belong to Christ, verily I say unto you, **he shall not lose his reward.**

Everyone who works for the Lord is going to receive some type of Reward, and we are told that the Rewards we receive will be according to our labor. In other words, Christians who work harder and accomplish more for the Kingdom can expect to receive a greater reward than those who work little.

1 Corinthians 3:8 Now he that planteth and he that watereth are one: and **every man shall receive his own reward according to his own labour.**

We are told to be diligent in our work so that we don't lose anything that we could have had. We are told we should try to receive our full reward.

2 John 1:8 Look to yourselves, that we lose not those things which we have wrought, **but that we receive a full reward**.

Jesus is going to give us our Rewards when we stand before Him at the Judgement Seat of Christ. All Christians will stand before Jesus at this Judgement Seat.

> Romans 14:10 But why dost thou judge thy brother? or why dost thou set at nought thy brother? **for we shall all stand before the judgment seat of Christ.**

It's at this Judgement Seat that the Christian will see both good things they have done in their life that benefited the Kingdom, as well as the bad things they've done. Many of us will want to hang our heads low when we see some of the stupid and selfish things we have done in the flesh, and we will wish we had done more for Jesus.

> 2 Corinthians 5:10 <u>For we must all appear before the judgment seat of Christ</u>; **that every one may receive the things done in his body**, according to that he hath done, whether it be good or bad.

At this time, everyone's works will be made manifest which means they will be revealed. Furthermore, they will be tried by fire to see what sore they are. This means God is going to reveal not only what we've done, but He's going to look at our intentions. For instance, if someone gives money to a church so they can get recognition, that person won't receive the reward that someone else who gives for the correct intention will receive.

> 1 Corinthians 3:13 <u>Every man's work shall be made manifest</u>: for the day shall declare it, because it shall be revealed by fire; and **the fire shall <u>try every man's work of what sort it is</u>**.

Whatever work we have that makes it through this fire will be rewarded!

---

1 Corinthians 3:14 **If any man's work abide** which he hath built thereupon, **he shall receive a reward**.

Some Christians will not have any work that makes it through the fire. Some will stand before Jesus and see that they wasted their lives living selfishly instead of working for the Kingdom. They'll see that everything they lived for, stressed about, and dreamed about went up in smoke because it wasn't for God's Kingdom. Nevertheless, the person will be saved even though they have nothing they've done worthy of reward!

---

1 Corinthians 3:15 <u>If any man's work shall be burned</u>, <u>he shall suffer loss</u>: **but he himself shall be saved**; yet so as by fire.

One might ask, what type of Rewards is God going to give to His people? We are told that we can't even imagine what God has planned for us. When we are in Eternity, what we experience will be beyond anything that's ever been seen, heard about, or thought of!

1 Corinthians 2:9 But as it is written, Eye hath not seen, nor ear heard, neither have entered into the heart of man, the things which God hath prepared for them that love him.	Isaiah 64:4 For since the beginning of the world men have not heard, nor perceived by the ear, neither hath the eye seen, O God, beside thee, what he hath prepared for him that waiteth for him.

However, God does reveal to us what one type of Reward is going to be. One way in which He'll reward us is by giving us a Crown. This is the type of Crown that is worn by a King or a Queen. The Bible describes 5 different Crowns that are available and that are given as Rewards to the Believer.

The First Crown the New Testament speaks of is what some refer to as the <u>Crown of Victory</u>. The Apostle Paul tells us that he was trying to receive this Crown. This Crown only goes to a small number of Believers. What was Paul doing to try to achieve this Crown? For one, Paul didn't receive payment for his preaching of the Gospel. This doesn't mean it's wrong for a Pastor to receive a salary. As a matter of fact, the Bible supports recompensing those who work for the Lord. Paul, however, decided he'd rather make his ministry free so that all his reward would come from God, which is probably pretty smart on his part!

---

1 Corinthians 9:17 For if **I do this thing willingly, I have a reward**: but if against my will, a dispensation of the gospel is committed unto me

.

1 Corinthians 9:18 **What is my reward then**? Verily <u>that, when I preach the gospel, I may make the gospel of Christ without charge</u>, that I abuse not my power in the gospel.

Paul compares striving for this Crown to running a race. In his analogy, only one receives the prize. This lets us know that at most, few will receive this Crown.

---

1 Corinthians 9:24 Know ye not that they which run in a race run all, **but one receiveth the prize**? So run, that ye may obtain.

Paul then clarifies what the prize is. The prize is a Crown. The crown that is received in his analogy is corruptible, such as what an athlete would receive. However, the Crown he is trying to get is Incorruptible which means it will never fade or decay.

> 1 Corinthians 9:25 And every man that striveth for the mastery is temperate in all things. Now **they do it to obtain a corruptible crown; but we an incorruptible.**

Paul continues and says that he is like a runner training for a race and like a fighter who beats the air (such as a boxer shadow-boxing).

> 1 Corinthians 9:26 I therefore so run, not as uncertainly; so fight I, not as one that beateth the air:

You see, to receive this Crown you have to train yourself to deny yourself, such as when Paul didn't accept money for his preaching. The Crown of Victory goes to someone who is victorious over their fleshly desires and pleasures of this current world. Paul knew that if he didn't keep his bodily desires and lust in check, he wouldn't receive this Crown. Paul says that if he wasn't careful, he would be a castaway or rejected. Sadly, some people take this verse out of context to try to convince someone they can lose their Salvation if they don't work hard to keep it. This has nothing to do with losing Salvation. Paul is referring here to the Crown of Victory!

> 1 Corinthians 9:27 But I keep under my body, and bring it into subjection: lest that by any means, when I have preached to others, I myself should be a castaway.

The Second Crown that is spoken of is the <u>Crown of Rejoicing</u>. This Crown is also referred to as the Soul Winners Crown. The Bible says that Heaven and God Himself rejoice when a Soul is saved.

Luke 15:10 Likewise, I say unto you, **there is joy in the presence of the angels of God over one sinner that repenteth.**	Zephaniah 3:17 The LORD thy God in the midst of thee is mighty; **he will save, he will rejoice over thee with joy**; he will rest in his love, he will joy over thee with singing.

The Bible tells us it's a wise thing to win souls. Those who win souls will someday shine like the stars!

Proverbs 11:30 The fruit of the righteous is a tree of life; and **he that winneth souls is wise.**	Daniel 12:3 And **they that be wise shall shine** as the brightness of the firmament; and **they that turn many to righteousness as the stars for ever and ever.**

Paul told the Philippians that they were his crown and the Thessalonians that they were his Crown of Rejoicing.

Philippians 4:1 Therefore, my brethren dearly beloved and longed for, **my joy and crown**, so stand fast in the Lord, my dearly beloved.	1 Thessalonians 2:19 For what is our hope, or joy, **or crown of rejoicing**? Are not even ye in the presence of our Lord Jesus Christ at his coming?

The Crown of Rejoicing will be given to those who win Souls to the Lord.

The Third Crown that we read about is the Crown of Righteousness. Jesus tells us that those who long for Righteousness are blessed.

Matthew 5:6 Blessed are they which do hunger and thirst after righteousness: for they shall be filled.

In its current state, the Earth is full of sin and cursed. However, when Jesus returns, He is going to restore Righteousness in the Earth. In the Lord's Prayer, we are shown that we should pray for this day and desire it.

Matthew 6:10 Thy kingdom come, **Thy will be done in earth, as it is in heaven.**

Paul told Timothy that he was going to receive a Crown of Righteousness. Paul also says that this Crown won't be given to him alone, but to all those who love the Lord's appearance.

2 Timothy 4:8 Henceforth there is laid up for me **a crown of righteousness**, which the Lord, the righteous judge, shall give me at that day: and not to me only, but unto all them also that love his appearing.

The Crown of Righteousness will be given to those who are longing for the Lord to return and bring Righteousness back to the Earth. It is for those who are burdened by this sinful world and can't wait for the Lord to make things right. It's not for those who want the Lord to come back someday, just not today… Rather, it's for those who hunger and thirst for Him to return.

The Fourth Crown is the Crown of Life. Jesus tells us that we should expect trials and tribulations in this world. We should also expect persecution for being a Christian. When people hate you and don't want to be around you because of Jesus you are Blessed!

Luke 6:22 **Blessed are ye, when men shall hate you**, and when they shall separate you from their company, and shall reproach you, and cast out your name as evil, **for the Son of man's sake**.

How is that a blessing you may ask? If you're a true Christian and you don't go along with the World or agree with their ways, they'll hate you. The reason you're blessed is because Jesus is going to Reward you for acting like a Real Christian! Jesus has a Great Reward waiting for those who "walk the walk" rather than just "talk the talk".

Luke 6:23 **Rejoice ye in that day, and leap for joy**: for, behold, **your reward is great in heaven:** for in the like manner did their fathers unto the prophets.

James shows us that one of the Rewards we'll receive when enduring this type of temptation is the Crown of Life. If we truly love Jesus, we'll be motivated to live for Him. The more we love Him, the less we'll care about having the world's approval, and the less we'll fear what man can do to us.

James 1:12 Blessed is the man that endureth temptation: for **when he is tried, he shall receive the crown of life**, which the Lord hath promised to them that love him.

It's one thing to live for the Lord when there's not much persecution. It's another thing when being a Christian literally threatens your life. A lot of us have been fortunate enough to live in a place where we haven't had to face this level of persecution, but our brethren in other places have and do every day. When a person dies for the Lord's sake it's a very precious thing to Him.

Psalm 116:15 **Precious** in the sight of the LORD **is the death of his saints.**	Psalm 72:14 He shall redeem their soul from deceit and violence: **and precious shall their blood be in his sight.**

The Lord promises that those who are faithful to Him even to the point of losing their physical life, will be given the Crown of Life.

Revelation 2:10 **Fear none of those things which thou shalt suffer:** behold, the devil shall cast some of you into prison, that ye may be tried; and ye shall have tribulation ten days: **be thou faithful unto death, and I will give thee a crown of life.**

The Fifth Crown is the <u>Crown of Glory</u>. Jesus is our Great Shepard, but He's also given the church a local Pastor, who is also a shepherd. These men have a great responsibility to help feed the Lord's flock (His people). The Lord tells them to do their work willingly and not for money.

1 Peter 5:2 **Feed the flock of God** which is among you, taking the oversight thereof, not by constraint, but **willingly; not for filthy lucre**, but of a ready mind;

They are supposed to be good examples to the flock, and they are not to lord over them, which means they don't make the flock think they are their masters or that they should serve them.

> 1 Peter 5:3 Neither as being lords over God's heritage, but being examples to the flock.

The Pastors who feed their flocks and do what the Lord requires will receive a Crown of Glory.

> 1 Peter 5:4 And <u>when the chief Shepherd shall appear</u>, **ye shall receive a crown of glory** that fadeth not away.

A Summary of the 5 Crowns.

The Crown	Received by
The Crown of Victory	Those who deny their flesh in order to better serve the Lord
The Crown of Rejoicing	Those who win souls to the Lord
The Crown of Righteousness	Those who long for the Lord to return in Righteousness
The Crown of Life	Those who endure temptations and tribulation even unto death
The Crown of Glory	Those who shepherd the Lord's flock

When Jesus was crucified, the soldiers placed a Crown of Thorns on His head. They mocked the One who created them by putting a purple robe on Him, which signified royalty, and by placing the crown on His head.

John 19:2 And the soldiers platted **a crown of thorns**, and put it on his head, and they put on him a purple robe,

Jesus wore a Crown of Thorns so He could give you a Crown of Gold! King David speaks of the Golden Crown. This is not a manmade crown but the Crown that the Lord will give him.

Psalm 21:1 The king shall joy in thy strength, O LORD; and in thy salvation how greatly shall he rejoice!

Psalm 21:3 For thou preventest him with the blessings of goodness: **thou settest a crown of pure gold on his head**.

None of us are worthy of a crown. Actually, there is one crown we are worthy of, which is the Crown of Thorns. Only Jesus deserves to wear a Crown of Pure Gold. The 24 Elders spoken of in Revelation realize this, and that is why they cast their crowns before the Lord.

Revelation 4:10 The four and twenty elders fall down before him that sat on the throne, and worship him that liveth for ever and ever, and **cast their crowns before the throne**, saying,

Revelation 4:11 **Thou art worthy, O Lord**, to receive glory and honour and power: for thou hast created all things, and for thy pleasure they are and were created.

When Jesus returns to Earth at the Second Coming, He's going to be wearing many Crowns. I don't know how many He'll be wearing but I think it will be at least 5!

> Revelation 19:12 His eyes were as a flame of fire, and **on his head were many crowns**; and he had a name written, that no man knew, but he himself.

Never forget that Salvation is a Free Gift from God. It can't be earned or worked for. It's not a Reward. However, also remember that there are Rewards that we should work for. If we're wise, we'll work hard to receive the Lord's Rewards. What the Lord wants to give you is far better than anything this world has to offer. Don't cheat yourself out of an Eternal Reward for some temporary pleasure. Don't let anyone take your Crown!

> Revelation 3:11 Behold, I come quickly: hold that fast which thou hast, **that no man take thy crown.**

The Sin Unto Death

The reason there are so many different Christian denominations is that most people are not willing to study the Bible. When reading a verse that contradicts what they believe, instead of reconciling the verses, they choose which verses to believe and which to ignore. Every Denomination can show you Bible verses that seem to confirm their beliefs. However, the only way to understand the Bible properly is to follow its instructions. God tells us that to understand His Doctrine, precept must be upon precept, and line upon line, here a little and there a little. This means when you read a precept in Genesis, that precept will hold true in Revelation. It is here a little and there a little. A little in Deuteronomy, a little in Romans, a little in Exodus, and a little in John.

Isaiah 28:9 **Whom shall he teach knowledge? and whom shall he make to understand doctrine**? them that are weaned from the milk, and drawn from the breasts.

Isaiah 28:10 For **precept must be upon precept**, precept upon precept; **line upon line**, line upon line; **here a little, and there a little**:

An example of precept upon precept is in the Gospel message itself. We see a precept in Genesis that shows us that when we sin, we die. That precept doesn't change anywhere in the Bible. We also see a precept in Genesis that God will provide a covering for sin. When Jesus died for our sins, He wasn't changing the precept. You see, Jesus took our place and died for us. Another precept that is learned in Genesis is that God accepts a Sacrifice for sin and Jesus was sacrificed for us. In the story of Abraham, we have a precept that shows us that God is willing to declare a person to be Righteous through Faith. Abraham was counted Righteous because he Trusted in the Lord and not because of any works he did.

The Bible is clear from Genesis to Revelation that Salvation is a Gift that is given through Faith apart from works. If that precept is not established in your heart, you may misinterpret several passages in the Bible. Also, you may come to believe that Salvation is achieved by being a good person, or you may think that while the death of Jesus was required as payment for your sins, it wasn't totally sufficient and that you must also contribute to your Salvation through your works and obedience. That belief is a false gospel.

A common passage in the Bible that is misinterpreted is in regard to the "Sin Unto Death". Some believe that God will have mercy on certain sins but that He will not have mercy on other sins. In other words, they think a Christian can commit lesser sins and still maintain their Salvation, but if they commit some greater sin (which is not defined by John) they could lose their Salvation.

> 1 John 5:16 If any man see his brother sin a sin which is not unto death, he shall ask, and he shall give him life for them that sin not unto death. **There is a sin unto death: I do not say that he shall pray for it.**

The question we must ask is, what sin is the Apostle John referring to? If there is a sin that could cause a Christian to lose their Salvation, don't you think John should have helped us out and told us what it was?? Furthermore, John says we shouldn't pray for someone who is committing this sin. If we don't know what sin the "Sin Unto Death" is, then how would we know whether or not we should pray for it??

Luckily, the Bible defines the Sin Unto Death for us. Shortly before the Jews were conquered by Babylon, God told Jeremiah not to pray for them! He told Jeremiah that if he prayed for them, He would not hear him!

> Jeremiah 7:16 Therefore **pray not thou for this people**, neither lift up cry nor prayer for them, neither make intercession to me: **for I will not hear thee**.

God explains why he told Jeremiah not to pray for them. He tells Jeremiah that He had spoken to them, but they wouldn't listen, and even after sending them many prophets they still refused to listen to Him.

> Jeremiah 7:24 But **they hearkened not**, nor inclined their ear, but walked in the counsels and in the imagination of their evil heart, and went backward, and not forward.
>
> Jeremiah 7:25 Since the day that your fathers came forth out of the land of Egypt unto this day **I have even sent unto you all my servants the prophets**, daily rising up early and sending them:

Then God tells Jeremiah, that even though he is going to also prophesy to them, they are not going to listen to Jeremiah either.

Jeremiah 7:27 Therefore **thou shalt speak all these words unto them; but they will not hearken to thee**: thou shalt also call unto them; but they will not answer thee.

Jeremiah continued to prophesy to the Jews and tell them everything that the Lord commanded him to say. However, once again God tells Jeremiah not to pray for them.

Jeremiah 11:14 **Therefore pray not thou for this people**, neither lift up a cry or prayer for them: for I will not hear them in the time that they cry unto me for their trouble.

Once again, God explains why Jeremiah is not to pray for them. He tells Jeremiah that He has spoken and protested to them, telling them to obey Him and not to follow other gods.

Jeremiah 11:7 **For I earnestly protested unto your fathers** in the day that I brought them up out of the land of Egypt, even unto this day, **rising early and protesting, saying, Obey my voice.**

But even though the Lord spoke to them, they refused to hear Him.

Jeremiah 11:10 They are turned back to the iniquities of their forefathers, **which refused to hear my words**; and they went after other gods to serve them: the house of Israel and the house of Judah have broken my covenant which I made with their fathers.

The reason that God told Jeremiah not to pray for the Jews is because He had clearly spoken to them and made His voice clear. You see, they understood the message. They had a clear understanding of what God's message was and yet they refused to listen! God wasn't going to force them to obey. They had to obey by their own free will.

Before we continue, we must understand something. Going to Church doesn't make anyone a Christian or a true believer. From the early days of the Church, there were false prophets and there were people in the Church who thought they were saved but were not. When the Apostles wrote letters to the churches they addressed the true church, but they also included warnings to those in the church who were not truly saved. Don't get caught up in the notion that because an apostle addresses a letter to the church, everything written applies to the true Born-Again believer because it doesn't. There are many in the church who are called Brothers or Sisters, but they are not true believers and Paul tells us not to have fellowship with these types of people.

> 1 Corinthians 5:11 But now I have written unto you not to keep company, **if any man that is called a brother** be a fornicator, or covetous, or an idolator, or a railer, or a drunkard, or an extortioner; with such an one no not to eat.

James shows us that there are people in the church who are called brethren who don't believe the truth and that by converting them, we assist in saving their souls! James is not referring to the truth of non-salvific issues such as whether the rapture is pre or post-trib. He is referring to the truth of the Gospel.

> James 5:19 **Brethren, if any of you do err from the truth**, and one convert him;
>
> James 5:20 Let him know, that **he which converteth the sinner from the error of his way shall save a soul from death**, and shall hide a multitude of sins.

The Apostles started churches, set up leaders in the local church, and then moved on to start other churches. They knew that after they left, false believers would come in, and false pastors whom they referred to as Wolves. Paul warned the Ephesians of these Wolves.

> Acts 20:29 For I know this, that after my departing shall grievous **wolves** enter in among you, not sparing the flock.

Peter and Jude both wrote about these Wolves in detail. Both Peter and Jude say that these Wolves are in ministry for money and compare them to Balaam from the Old Testament who was hired by the enemies of God to try to curse His people.

2 Peter 2:15 Which have forsaken the right way, and are gone astray, **following the way of Balaam the son of Bosor, who loved the wages of unrighteousness;**	Jude 11 Woe unto them! for they have gone in the way of Cain, and **ran greedily after the error of Balaam for reward,** and perished in the gainsaying of Core.

Peter and Jude both make it clear that these are unsaved individuals.

2 Peter 2:17 **These are wells without water**, clouds that are carried with a tempest; to whom the mist of darkness is reserved for ever.	Jude 19 **These be they** who separate themselves, sensual, **having not the Spirit**.

The Wolves deny Jesus and the True Gospel.

2 Peter 2:1 But there were false prophets also among the people, even as there shall be false teachers among you, **who privily shall bring in damnable heresies, even denying the Lord that bought them**, and bring upon themselves swift destruction.	Jude 4 For there are certain men crept in unawares, who were before of old ordained to this condemnation, ungodly men, turning the grace of our God into lasciviousness, **and denying the only Lord God, and our Lord Jesus Christ.**

The Wolves speak evil of the True Gospel, and they have many followers.

2 Peter 2:2 And many shall follow their pernicious ways; **by reason of whom the way of truth shall be evil spoken of.**

They lure people who have escaped from others living in error. For example, they lure someone who may have been hooked on drugs out of that lifestyle and promise them freedom and salvation.

2 Peter 2:18 For when they speak great swelling words of vanity, **they allure** through the lusts of the flesh, through much wantonness, those that were clean escaped from them who live in error.

However, while the Wolves promise freedom, they themselves are servants of Satan and of destruction.

2 Peter 2:19 **While they promise them liberty, they themselves are the servants of corruption**: for of whom a man is overcome, of the same is he brought in bondage.

Peter then tells us that these people who follow the Wolves are in a worse condition than if they'd never heard about Jesus!

> 2 Peter 2:20 For if after they have escaped the pollutions of the world through the knowledge of the Lord and Saviour Jesus Christ, they are again entangled therein, and overcome, **the latter end is worse with them than the beginning.**

You see, the Wolves claim to preach the correct gospel and they are very persuasive. However, the gospel they preach is False and will not save souls. The Wolf is mostly concerned with getting people's money. Because of that, they will focus mostly on prosperity and trying to link all of God's Blessings to tithing and giving. Of course, the Wolf takes the money for themselves, and in extreme cases, spends it on their lust such as multimillion-dollar homes and private jets. Peter goes on to explain that these people are turning from the Holy Commandment.

> 2 Peter 2:21 For it had been better for them not to have known the way of righteousness, than, after they have known it, **to turn from the holy commandment delivered unto them.**

What Holy Commandment are they turning from? They are turning from the Holy Commandment to Trust Jesus and Believe in Him alone for Salvation. This contradicts the Wolf's message which usually involves works for Salvation and denies the power of the New Birth.

> 1 John 3:23 And **this is his commandment, That we should believe on the name of his Son Jesus Christ**, and love one another, as he gave us commandment.

It's a dangerous thing to have a Holy Bible and to go to church all your life and not be Born Again! It's not that these people lost their Salvation. The problem is that instead of listening to God's Word, they listened to the Wolf instead. Why would they listen to the Wolf and trust what the Wolf says instead of the True Gospel? The Bible says the Wolves deceive the hearts of the Simple.

Romans 16:18 For they that are such serve not our Lord Jesus Christ, but their own belly; and **by good words and fair speeches deceive the hearts of the simple.**

Who are the Simple? The Bible defines who the Simple is. The Simple are those who believe what the Wolf tells them without searching the matter out. Instead of reading their Bible to see if what the Wolf is saying is true, they blindly follow what the Wolf says.

Proverbs 14:15 **The simple believeth every word**: but the prudent man looketh well to his going.

The people who follow the Wolves are like dogs and pigs. You can put clothes on a dog but it's still a dog. You can wash a pig and put a dress and lipstick on it to make it look pretty, but the pig will still jump in a mud puddle because it's a pig! Dogs and Pigs are unclean animals and do what they do because of their nature. These people never had a change of Nature.

2 Peter 2:22 But it is happened unto them according to the true proverb, **The dog is turned to his own vomit again; and the sow that was washed to her wallowing in the mire.**

Someone who is truly Born-Again has a new Nature. The New Nature is given to us by God when we're saved and it's Him that gives us the power to live Holy. We're not pigs and dogs that have been given a bath, but we are new creatures who partake in God's Holy Nature!

2 Peter 1:3 According as **his divine power hath given unto us all things that pertain unto life and godliness,** through the knowledge of him that hath called us to glory and virtue:

2 Peter 1:4 Whereby are given unto us exceeding great and precious promises: that by these **ye might be partakers of the divine nature,** having escaped the corruption that is in the world through lust.

So, what is the Sin Unto Death? The Sin Unto Death is turning away from God's message of Salvation after having a clear understanding of it. Most people don't understand the Gospel, even people who've been in church all their lives. When we realize someone who is called a brother or sister is not following the truth, we are supposed to present the True Gospel to them and try to help them understand it. If they don't understand it, we should pray for God to help them understand. This applies to someone outside the church as well.

However, if the issue is not that they don't understand, but rather they understand but simply reject the message, then we shouldn't pray for God to make them Trust in Him. God will not violate someone's free will and make them put their Trust in Him. He won't flip a switch in their hearts and cause them to believe. I've prayed many times for God to make someone believe the Gospel, and most of us with lost loved ones will do this.

However, we must realize that if God flipped a switch in our loved one's hearts and made them believe, then He'd be obligated to flip everyone's switch and make everyone believe, and He simply will not do that. He gives everyone the choice to put their Trust in Him. He gives us free will and wants us to willingly choose to Believe and Trust Him. He wants a real loving relationship and not something that is forced upon someone.

I told you it's a dangerous thing to have a Holy Bible and to go to church and not be Born Again. God will hold a person who has access to the truth much more accountable on judgment day than someone who didn't have much access to it. We must make our calling and election sure. We must make sure we understand the true Gospel and follow it, and that we don't blindly follow a Wolf. When a person understands God's message and the Gospel of Jesus Christ but turns from it, they will remain in the Congregation of the Dead. Instead of the Dead Person being Born-Again and given Life, the Dead remains with the Dead.

> Proverbs 21:16 The man that wandereth out of the way of understanding **shall remain in the congregation of the dead**.

They don't leave the Congregation of the Living because they were never a part of that Congregation. Rather, they remain where they are, which is with the Dead. This is the Sin Unto Death.

Preserved by the Lord

If the Lord forgave us of all our past sins and mistakes, that alone would be a great mercy. It's a great kindness to give someone a second chance. King David realized that God had shown him mercy and that He had saved his soul from Hell.

> Psalm 86:13 For great is thy mercy toward me: and thou hast delivered my soul from the lowest hell.

However, our problem is that as long as we're still in a body of flesh and blood, we're not perfect. We still have some magnitude of sin in our lives even after being Born Again. If it were up to us to keep ourselves saved, we wouldn't remain saved for one day! So, we need the Lord to not only save us from our past sins, but we need Him to preserve us, and to keep us in relationship with Him. King David realized this, and He asked God if He would keep him saved.

> Psalm 56:13 <u>For thou hast delivered my soul from death</u>: **wilt not thou deliver my feet from falling**, that I may walk before God in the light of the living?

Now, Hannah who was the Prophet Samuel's mother, had previously had a revelation. Hannah said that God would keep the feet of His saints. She also made a statement that by strength a man would not prevail. What Hannah was saying is that a man could not find or keep Salvation in his own power.

> 1 Samuel 2:9 **He will keep the feet of his saints**, and the wicked shall be silent in darkness; for **by strength shall no man prevail**.

God continued to speak to David and revealed to him that He would hold David's hand. This means that God is going to be with David and is going to be always holding on to him.

> Psalm 73:23 Nevertheless I am continually with thee: **thou hast holden me by my right hand.**

God has promised to hold our hand as well.

> Isaiah 41:13 For I the LORD thy God **will hold thy right hand**, saying unto thee, Fear not; **I will help thee**.

This didn't mean that David would never fall. He would fall at times. However, because God is holding David's hand, he would not be utterly cast down.

> Psalm 37:24 <u>Though he fall, he shall not be utterly cast down</u>: **for the LORD upholdeth him with his hand.**

David knew that the Lord would uphold others as well. He knew this grace would not only be extended to him but to all those who belonged to the Lord.

> Psalm 145:14 **The LORD upholdeth all that fall**, and raiseth up all those that be bowed down.

A Just Man (a person declared righteous by the Lord) may fall many times. However, because God is holding our hand, we'll get back up!

> Proverbs 24:16 **For a just man falleth seven times, and riseth up again**: but the wicked shall fall into mischief.

By the time David wrote Psalm 116, he had received the answer he was looking for. He knew that God was going to keep him.

Psalm 56:13 <u>For thou hast delivered my soul from death</u>: **wilt not thou deliver my feet from falling**, that I may walk before God in the light of the living?	Psalm 116:8 <u>For thou hast delivered my soul from death,</u> mine eyes from tears, **and my feet from falling**.

It was the Lord who preserved David and kept him. David wasn't keeping himself in his own power. The Lord held David's hand and didn't let him go. The Lord Jesus told us that when He holds our hand, no one will pluck us away or out of His Hand. Once He has you, He intends to hang on!

John 10:28 **And I give unto them eternal life; and they shall never perish**, neither shall any man pluck them out of my hand.

John 10:29 My Father, which gave them me, is greater than all; and **no man is able to pluck them out of my Father's hand**.

When Jesus saves us, He begins working on us and through us! Remember, the Holy Ghost is inside of us giving us Life and Renewing us. Salvation is not a past experience but an ongoing work of the Lord. The good news is that when you're Born Again and the Lord starts His work on you, He's going to finish it!

Philippians 1:6 Being confident of this very thing, that **he which hath begun a good work in you will perform it until the day of Jesus Christ**:

It's the Lord who is performing the work, not us. The Lord Jesus is our Advocate and High Priest. Because of Him, we are blameless in the eyes of God. We're promised that He will confirm us unto the end.

1 Corinthians 1:8 **Who shall also confirm you unto the end**, that ye may be blameless in the day of our Lord Jesus Christ.

When we arrive at the end, God will say we are unblameable and holy!

> 1 Thessalonians 3:13 **To the end he may stablish your hearts unblameable in holiness before God**, even our Father, at the coming of our Lord Jesus Christ with all his saints.

The reason God will call us Holy and unblameable is because our sins are covered by the Blood of Jesus. He has given us Christ's Righteousness; therefore, a sinner is seen as a saint who has no sin!

> Colossians 1:22 In the body of his flesh through death, **to present you holy and unblameable and unreproveable in his sight:**

The Lord is at work right now preserving us. Remember, He promised in Isaiah that He would hold our hand. He is Faithful to do what He says!

> 1 Thessalonians 5:23 And the very God of peace sanctify you wholly; and I pray God your whole spirit and soul and body **be preserved blameless unto the coming of our Lord Jesus Christ.**
>
> 1 Thessalonians 5:24 **Faithful is he that calleth you, who also will do it.**

The Lord is able and has promised to Preserve us. It is Him that keeps our feet from falling. Though we may fall temporarily, He holds us in His Hand and pulls us back up.

Psalm 116:8 For thou hast delivered my soul from death, mine eyes from tears, **and my feet from falling**.	Jude 24 **Now unto him that is able to keep you from falling**, and to present you faultless before the presence of his glory with exceeding joy,

God foresees all those who will Believe in Him and come to Salvation. In other words, He knows what's going to happen before it happens. God calls those people to Himself through Faith in Jesus. When we Trust in Jesus and are born-again, we are given to Jesus and become Children of Christ or Children of the Lord. We are promised that the Lord will never cast us away when this happens!

John 6:37 All that the Father giveth me shall come to me; and him that cometh to me I will in no wise cast out.

Jesus tells us that He was sent to accomplish the Father's will.

John 6:38 For I came down from heaven, not to do mine own will, but the will of him that sent me.

Jesus then tells us that it's the will of the Father that Jesus will not lose anyone who the Father has given Him! Moreover, not only will Jesus not lose anyone who was given to Him, but He will raise them up on the last day, which is the last day of the current age of time we're living in. Notice, Jesus is the One who is accomplishing this. This isn't us hanging on to Jesus, but it's Jesus hanging on to us and carrying us through to the end! If any truly Born-Again person were to lose their salvation, then Jesus would fail in accomplishing the Father's will. Of course, that won't happen, and Jesus will perform the will of the Father!

> John 6:39 And **this is the Father's will** which hath sent me, that of all which he hath given me **I should lose nothing,** but should raise it up again at the last day.

It's God's Power that saves us and keeps us saved. God promised to do this in the Old Testament as well as the New Testament. Jesus prayed that the Father would keep those given to Him through His own name. The entire Godhead is active in keeping us saved!

> John 17:11 And now I am no more in the world, but these are in the world, and I come to thee. **Holy Father, keep through thine own name those whom thou hast given me**, that they may be one, as we are.

The Father answered the prayer of the Son, and He keeps all those who belong to Him. Peter realized that we are kept by the Power of God.

> 1 Peter 1:5 **Who are kept by the power of God** through faith unto salvation ready to be revealed in the last time.

God is going to preserve His saints forever. To preserve something is to keep it from spoiling or free from decay. It also means to keep something alive. It means to keep something from perishing. Those who have been Born Again will Never Perish. We are Preserved Forever!

Psalm 37:28 For the LORD loveth judgment, and forsaketh not **his saints; they are preserved for ever**: but the seed of the wicked shall be cut off.

What God does will last Forever

Salvation is a complete work of God. It's God who saves us and keeps us saved. Someone who is Born-Again doesn't get saved through any act of themselves. The Bible says we are not born of blood which means we aren't born again through our bloodline, such as being Jewish etc. We are not born again through the will of the flesh, which means we can't decide in our flesh that we're going to be saved, and then perform some work such as walking an aisle or being water baptized. Also, we are not born again through the will of man, which among other things means that no one can pray you into Heaven or into a saved condition. The Bible says we are Born-Again through the will of God, which means Salvation is a work that God alone does.

John 1:13 **Which were born**, not of blood, nor of the will of the flesh, nor of the will of man, but **of God**.

The Apostle James tells us that God begat us, which means born us unto Himself, through the Word of Truth. The Word of Truth is the Gospel of Jesus. It's by Trusting in Jesus that we are saved and it's God who initiates this and begets us. We are Born Again as His children entirely by His power.

> James 1:18 **Of his own will begat he us with the word of truth**, that we should be a kind of firstfruits of his creatures.

When God saves us, He places a seed in our hearts which grows and produces fruit. It also grows into a "New Man" and a new creature. The seed that takes root in our hearts is the Gospel message and is the Word of God. Jesus reveals to us that the seed is the Word of God.

> Luke 8:11 Now the parable is this: **The seed is the word of God**.

When we are born into this world we are born of a corruptible seed. We are born of flesh and blood, and because we sin, we eventually perish and die. However, when we are Born of God, we are born of an incorruptible seed! This means that the "New Man" which is our born-again spirit man, cannot be corrupted!

> 1 Peter 1:23 **Being born again, not of corruptible seed, but of incorruptible**, by the word of God, which liveth and abideth for ever.

Peter shows us that the old man who is born of the corruptible seed will perish and wither away just like grass does. This is our flesh.

> 1 Peter 1:24 For **all flesh is as grass**, and all the glory of man as the flower of grass. **The grass withereth**, and the flower thereof falleth away:

However, the Word of the Lord, which is the incorruptible seed, will never perish. This means the "New Man" can never perish because he is born from that seed!

1 Peter 1:25 But **the word of the Lord endureth for ever**. And this is **the word which by the gospel** is preached unto you.	Isaiah 40:8 <u>The grass withereth, the flower fadeth</u>: but **the word of our God shall stand for ever.**

Remember that after we are Born Again, we must still struggle in our Flesh as long as we are in our natural bodies. The Flesh is our Old Man. The Old Man is corrupt because he is born of the corruptible seed. The Apostle Paul shows us that we need to stop listening to the "Old Man".

> Ephesians 4:22 That ye **put off** concerning the former conversation **the old man, which is corrupt** according to the deceitful lusts;

We should be renewed in our minds by the spirit of our new man.

> Ephesians 4:23 And be renewed in the spirit of your mind;

We do this by putting on the New Man, or in other words walking in the Spirit. When we live our lives focusing on the Lord and His Word and listening to His voice, we are putting on the New Man and walking in the Spirit. Now, notice the New Man is created by God and is righteous and holy!

> Ephesians 4:24 And that ye put on **the new man**, which after God **is created in righteousness and true holiness.**

The Apostle John shows us that the New Man cannot sin! The reason the New Man cannot sin is because he is created from the incorruptible seed and the seed remains in him! The New Man is born of God and is not capable of sinning!

> 1 John 3:9 Whosoever is born of God doth not commit sin; for **his seed remaineth in him**: and he cannot sin, because he is born of God.

Am I saying that a Born-Again Christian can't sin? No! Remember, we have a dual nature. We have an Old Man, and we have a New Man. In our flesh we still sin at times, however, the New Man who is our born-again spirit doesn't sin. This is why Paul said that when he sinned it wasn't him that was sinning but sin that dwelled in him. He is referring to the sin that is in his flesh or in his Old Man.

> Romans 7:17 Now then **it is no more I that do it**, but sin that dwelleth in me.
>
> Romans 7:20 Now if I do that I would not, it is no more I that do it, **but sin that dwelleth in me**.

Paul shows us that the New Man delights in God's Law. The Inward Man that Paul refers to is the same as the New Man which is the Born-Again spiritual man.

> Romans 7:22 For I delight in the law of God after the inward man:

Paul understands that his Old Man will always be a servant to sin. You will never fully conquer sin in your flesh. However, the New Man that is created by God through the incorruptible seed, serves God and His Law.

> Romans 7:25 I thank God through Jesus Christ our Lord. So then **with the mind I myself serve the law of God**; but with the flesh the law of sin.

Satan can touch and afflict the Old Man. Because of our sin, our flesh is subject to decay, and it dies. However, we are promised that the New Man will not be touched by that wicked one! Our New Man is Born of God and does not sin! The Spirit of the Born Again person does not sin but keeps itself through the power of God.

> 1 John 5:18 We know that **whosoever is born of God** sinneth not; but **he that is begotten of God keepeth himself,** and that wicked one toucheth him not.

Jesus is the only One who was sinless in the flesh. When Jesus lived His life free from sin, He overcame the power of Satan and of the world.

> John 16:33 These things I have spoken unto you, that in me ye might have peace. In the world ye shall have tribulation: but be of good cheer; **I have overcome the world.**

The Bible tells us that whoever is Born Again also overcomes the world thru faith in Jesus.

> 1 John 5:4 For **whatsoever is born of God overcometh the world**: and this is **the victory that overcometh the world, even our faith**.

False Religion which includes many who call themselves Christians, try to get the Old Man good enough to make it to Heaven. This is sad because they'll never get the Old Man to be good enough. They don't realize that you must be perfect to get to Heaven. We are Perfect in Jesus. It's our New Man who is saved and going to glory. The Old Man which is our flesh and blood cannot inherit God's Kingdom.

> 1 Corinthians 15:50 Now this I say, brethren, that **flesh and blood cannot inherit the kingdom of God**; neither doth corruption inherit incorruption.

Salvation is an act of God! It will last forever. It's God who begets us and by whom we are Born-Again. We are Born Again through God's incorruptible seed. Nothing can be added to it, and nothing can be taken away from it. The New Man will NEVER die!

> Ecclesiastes 3:14 I know that, **whatsoever God doeth, it shall be for ever**: nothing can be put to it, nor any thing taken from it: and God doeth it, that men should fear before him.

The Lord Knows Those Who Are His

Before God created the world, He foreknew those who would put their Trust in Him. In other words, God knew before you were born whether your heart would be willing to Trust Him and to Believe the Gospel. God knows who belongs to Him and who is playing religion. So, as He says in Nahum, He knows those who Trust in Him.

> Nahum 1:7 The LORD is good, a strong hold in the day of trouble; and **he knoweth them that trust in him**.

When the Lord speaks of knowing someone, He isn't just referring to the fact that He has knowledge of them. To know the Lord and for the Lord to know you means He has a personal relationship with you. All Born Again Christians have a personal relationship with the Lord. Many people think they are saved and know the Lord through their religion. Sadly, if there's no personal relationship, the Lord will someday tell them "I Never Knew You".

In the Old Covenant, the knowledge of God was taught by men from generation to generation. Moses delivered the law to Israel, and they were to teach it to their children. Those who took the law to heart would have a mark so to speak which would identify them. This sign or mark would be in their hands which indicates a person's work or actions, and it would be in their forehead, between their eyes, which would indicate that it directed their vision or focus.

Deuteronomy 6:7 And **thou shalt teach them diligently** unto thy children, and shalt talk of them when thou sittest in thine house, and when thou walkest by the way, and when thou liest down, and when thou risest up.

Deuteronomy 6:8 And thou shalt bind them for **a sign upon thine hand**, and they shall be **as frontlets between thine eyes**.

The problem Israel had with the Old Covenant was that keeping the Covenant relied upon the strength of the flesh. In order to know God and have a relationship with Him, Israel had to keep His laws. Joshua and the people who entered the Promised Land served the Lord during Joshua's life. However, in one generation, Israel went from serving the Lord to not Knowing Him.

Judges 2:10 And also all that generation were gathered unto their fathers: and there arose another generation after them, **which knew not the LORD**, nor yet the works which he had done for Israel.

During the time of the Judges, Israel had trouble after trouble. It seemed like the Covenant was hanging by a tread because the Lord would raise up a Judge who would help Israel get back on the right track, but then they would fall away again and again. They would stop trusting in the Lord and follow other gods. It wasn't until the days of David that Israel seemed to wholly follow the Lord. David trusted the Lord and had a personal relationship with Him, and he led Israel to trust in and follow the Lord. David said that those who know the Lord and trust Him are God's people and His sheep.

> Psalm 100:3 Know ye that the LORD he is God: it is he that hath made us, and not we ourselves; **we are his people, and the sheep of his pasture.**

After David died, Israel fell away again. It seemed like things were going well, and they were, under the rule of Solomon. However, Solomon committed acts of idolatry in order to please his wives and this eventually led to the Kingdom of Israel being split. Eventually, God had enough, and hundreds of years later the Kingdom was lost. Still, God had a remnant of people who trusted in Him and had a relationship with Him after the manner of David and Abraham, which was based on Faith. So, God promised that He was going to establish a New Covenant with Israel. However, unlike the Old Covenant, knowing God would not rely on the strength of the flesh. God promised that everyone who was a part of this Covenant was going to Know Him! From the least to the greatest says God.

Jeremiah 31:34 And **they shall teach no more** every man his neighbour, and every man his brother, saying, **Know the LORD: for they shall all know me, from the least of them unto the greatest of them,** saith the LORD: for I will forgive their iniquity, and I will remember their sin no more.	Hebrews 8:11 And they shall not teach every man his neighbour, and every man his brother, saying, **Know the Lord: for all shall know me, from the least to the greatest.**

Remember, David said that God's people are His sheep. Jesus tells us that when we Trust in Him, we are His sheep. Furthermore, Jesus tells us that when we are His sheep, we will Know Him and He will Know us!

John 10:14 I am the good shepherd, and **know my sheep**, and **am known of mine.**

Those who are the Lord's sheep hear His voice and they follow Him.

John 10:27 My sheep hear my voice, **and I know them**, and **they follow me:**

When someone Trusts in the Lord, God puts a mark upon them. Ezekial had a vision, and in the vision, God said to put a mark on the forehead of everyone who mourned for the evil things going on in Jerusalem at the time.

Ezekiel 9:4 And the LORD said unto him, Go through the midst of the city, through the midst of Jerusalem, and **set a mark upon the foreheads of the men that sigh and that cry** for all the abominations that be done in the midst thereof.

As I said, this was a vision. However, it is a picture of what God does and how He marks those who Trust in Him. The mark is not physical or at least something we can see with the physical eye, but I believe it's something that angels and demons can see. The mark lets angelic powers know they need to spare the person from wrath among other things. Another example of this is found in Revelation, where the angels are told to seal the 144,000 in their foreheads before they begin to pour out wrath on the earth.

> Revelation 7:3 Saying, Hurt not the earth, neither the sea, nor the trees, **till we have sealed the servants of our God in their foreheads**.

Satan will often try to mimic God. During the Tribulation, Satan will also mark people in their hands and foreheads. This is famously known as the Mark of the Beast and will be instituted at the time of the Antichrist. We don't know for sure, but it seems that this mark will be physical and be able to be seen by men because it will dictate whether people can buy or sell. This is Satan's imitation of God's mark.

> Revelation 13:16 And he causeth all, both small and great, rich and poor, free and bond, **to receive a mark in their right hand, or in their foreheads:**

The Mark of the Beast will be the name of the Beast or Antichrist, or at least it will signify his name. Eventually, everyone is going to have one of two names on their foreheads, either Satan's name or God's.

We're shown that the seal whereby the 144,000 are sealed is the name of God.

> Revelation 14:1 And I looked, and, lo, a Lamb stood on the mount Sion, and with him an hundred forty and four thousand, **having his Father's name written in their foreheads.**

We're also shown that all the citizens of New Jerusalem will have our Father's name in our foreheads as well, so this isn't something exclusive to the 144,000!

> Revelation 22:4 And they shall see his face; and **his name shall be in their foreheads.**

The Bible shows us that all Born Again Believers are sealed. I used to think of this seal as the type of seal that would be on a jar. I would hope that nothing strong enough to pop the seal would come along. However, that's not the type of seal the Bible is referring to. The type of seal the Bible is referring to is a stamp or a mark of approval, and it's what a king would use. Kings would use this type of seal to certify something was from them and had their approval. It would ensure that the thing sealed got to its destination without being tampered with.

John 3:33 He that hath received his testimony hath **set to his seal** that God is true.	The person who believes the Gospel "sets to their seal" that God is true. This means the person certifies or gives their "Stamp of Approval" on God's message.

The Bible tells us that when we put our Trust in the Gospel we are sealed with the Holy Spirit! I used to think this read "sealed by the Holy Spirit". However, it's not by but with. In other words, the Seal is the Holy Spirit Himself! The Holy Spirit is God's Stamp of Approval on the Believer.

> Ephesians 1:13 <u>In whom ye also trusted</u>, after that ye heard the word of truth, <u>the gospel of your salvation</u>: in whom also <u>after that ye believed</u>, **ye were sealed with that holy Spirit of promise,**

God marks or stamps the Believer with The Holy Spirit, which is His Seal of Approval. The Seal, which is the Holy Spirit, is our earnest or downpayment that God has placed upon us. God purchased our souls with His blood on the cross. An earnest payment is something that a buyer gives as a good faith deposit, which shows his intention to complete the purchase. God gives us His Holy Spirit as an earnest deposit which shows us that He intends to complete the deal, which is our total redemption.

> Ephesians 1:14 **Which is the earnest** of our inheritance **until the redemption of the purchased possession**, unto the praise of his glory.

One of the New Covenant promises is that God will put His fear into the hearts of His believers. This fear will prevent the believer from departing from Him. This is not a maybe, it is a New Covenant fact and a promise from God.

> Jeremiah 32:40 And I will make an everlasting covenant with them, that I will not turn away from them, to do them good; but **I will put my fear in their hearts, that they shall not depart from me.**

Among other things, this is one of the reasons that the Apostle John knew that those who had departed the faith were never really part of the true church. They were never truly Born Again.

> 1 John 2:19 They went out from us, but they were not of us; for **if they had been of us, they would no doubt have continued with us**: but they went out, that they might be made manifest that they were not all of us.

The New Testament scriptures explain how God keeps us from departing from Him. We know He puts His fear in us, but He explains this in further detail in the Epistles. First, we are told that God anoints us with the Holy Spirit. God anoints and seals us with His Holy Spirit.

> 2 Corinthians 1:21 Now he which stablisheth us with you in Christ, **and hath anointed us**, is God;
>
> 2 Corinthians 1:22 **Who hath also sealed us**, and given the earnest of the Spirit in our hearts.

We are then told that the anointing we receive, which is the Holy Spirit, remains in us and teaches us. He leads us into truth in all things. He also teaches and causes us to remain in the faith, and to abide in Jesus. Because of the work of the Holy Spirit, we shall abide in Jesus. Not that we could or should, but we shall, or in other words Will!

> 1 John 2:27 But **the anointing which ye have received of him abideth in you**, and ye need not that any man teach you: but as the same anointing teacheth you of all things, and is truth, and is no lie, and **even as it hath taught you, ye shall abide in him.**

Jesus told us that when the Comforter comes to us, which is the Holy Spirit also called the Holy Ghost, He will abide with us forever. We will know Him and He will be with us and in us.

> John 14:16 And I will pray the Father, and he shall give you another Comforter, that **he may abide with you for ever**;
>
> John 14:17 Even the Spirit of truth; whom the world cannot receive, because it seeth him not, neither knoweth him: **but ye know him**; for he dwelleth with you, and shall be in you.

But what if we sin, you may ask? How can the Holy Spirit remain with us when we fall short and sin. The Bible says that it grieves the Holy Spirit when we sin. Although it causes Him grief, He suffers through it and remains with us, because God has sealed us unto the day of redemption. Note, He doesn't say until, He says unto. The reason it's important to make that distinction is because God has made His Seal to be Unto Redemption. In other words, the Seal will not and cannot be broken! The Holy Spirit will carry the Believer to Redemption and Nothing will stop Him from accomplishing His purpose!

> Ephesians 4:30 And grieve not the holy Spirit of God, whereby **ye are sealed unto the day of redemption.**

True Born-Again Believers are eternally Sealed by God. He has anointed us with His Holy Spirit. I believe when the Father looks at us, He sees the name of Jesus in our foreheads. Those who receive the Mark of the Beast will be eternally damned. Those who receive the Mark of the Lamb will be Eternally Saved!

Sometimes this can be hard to believe. We see so many people who were once religious and seemed to be Christians who fall away. If you're not careful this can make you doubt some of the promises of God. Paul and Timothy were dealing with this in their day. Paul warned Timothy about a couple of Heretics in the church who were overthrowing some of the church member's faith. In other words, these two guys were preaching false doctrine and as a result, people were leaving the faith or leaving Jesus.

> 2 Timothy 2:17 And their word will eat as doth a canker: of whom is Hymenaeus and Philetus;
>
> 2 Timothy 2:18 Who concerning the truth have erred, saying that the resurrection is past already; **and overthrow the faith of some**.

However, Paul encourages Timothy and tells him that God's word is sure, in other words certain. Moreover, God's word has a seal or statement that says: The Lord Knows Those Who Are His! Some will fall away, however those who the Lord knows will remain with Him! This was an encouragement to Timothy, and it should be an encouragement to us as well. When the Lord saves you and places His deposit on you, you can be assured He's going to complete the deal!

> 2 Timothy 2:19 Nevertheless the foundation of God standeth sure, having this seal, **The Lord knoweth them that are his**. And, let every one that nameth the name of Christ depart from iniquity.

The Everlasting Covenant

They say that if something sounds too good to be true, it probably is. There is in fact a lot of wisdom to that statement and generally, you would be wise to follow that precept. On the other hand, a few things are "So Good That They Must Be True". The Gospel of Salvation is so good that it must be true because no sinful man could have invented that message. They say that nothing lasts forever. Again, generally, that's a good precept, but there are exceptions for there are things that are eternal. One of those eternal things is the Everlasting Covenant.

The Everlasting Covenant was first spoken of in Genesis. God established the Everlasting Covenant with Abraham. However, the Covenant was not unto Abraham alone, but it was to Abraham's descendants. In this Covenant, God promised to always be their God, and the land we now call Israel would always belong to Abraham's descendants. The word "Everlasting" means it will last forever. In other words, it's Eternal.

> Genesis 17:7 And I will establish my covenant between me and thee and thy seed after thee in their generations **for an everlasting covenant**, to be a God unto thee, and to thy seed after thee.

God made another Covenant with Moses and the children of Israel who followed Moses out of Egypt. However, this Covenant was Not an Everlasting Covenant. In this Covenant, God promised to bless Israel in the Promised Land if they followed His Law. God knew from the beginning that they would fail. God told Moses that some while after Moses died, Israel would forsake the Lord and break the Covenant.

> Deuteronomy 31:16 And the LORD said unto Moses, Behold, thou shalt sleep with thy fathers; and this people will rise up, and go a whoring after the gods of the strangers of the land, whither they go to be among them, **and will forsake me, and break my covenant** which I have made with them.

Then, God tells Moses that after Israel has forsaken Him and broken the Covenant, He will forsake them.

> Deuteronomy 31:17 Then my anger shall be kindled against them in that day, **and I will forsake them**, and I will hide my face from them, and they shall be devoured, and many evils and troubles shall befall them; so that they will say in that day, Are not these evils come upon us, because our God is not among us?

When you make an agreement or a Covenant with someone, terms must be laid out and agreed upon up-front. Let's say we make an agreement that I'll mow your yard for $50 and you sign a contract saying that I alone will mow your yard.

Now let's say I mow your yard and charge you $100. I tell you that I forgot to mention that I charge a $50 fuel surcharge on top of the $50 mowing fee. People do things just like this every day. Nevertheless, if I did that, I'd be breaking the contract because the contract we signed said nothing of a $50 fuel surcharge. When a Covenant is made between two parties, one party can't add to it without the other's consent.

> Galatians 3:15 Brethren, I speak after the manner of men; Though it be but a man's covenant, **yet if it be confirmed, no man disannulleth, or addeth thereto.**

When God made the Everlasting Covenant with Abraham, there was no mention of him or his descendants having to keep the Law. The Everlasting Covenant was made with Abraham and his Seed. Paul tells us that the Seed God was referring to was Jesus Christ.

> Galatians 3:16 Now **to Abraham and his seed were the promises made**. He saith not, And to seeds, as of many; but as of one, **And to thy seed, which is Christ.**

So, the Covenant that was made with Moses, which was according to the Law, could not void the Everlasting Covenant that was made between God and Abraham. The Law was given to Moses, not to Abraham.

> Galatians 3:17 And this I say, **that the covenant, that was confirmed before of God in Christ, the law,** which was four hundred and thirty years after, **cannot disannul**, that it should make the promise of none effect.

When we Trust in Jesus and are Born Again, we become Children of God, and we become spiritual descendants of Abraham. In other words, we become part of the Everlasting Covenant that God made with Abraham!

> Galatians 3:26 For ye are all the children of God by faith in Christ Jesus.
> Galatians 3:29 And **if ye be Christ's, then are ye Abraham's seed, and heirs according to the promise**.

Just as God told Moses, Israel broke the Covenant. God put up with them for hundreds of years and gave them time to repent, but they kept falling into idol worship and following other gods. Eventually, God had enough and declared the Covenant was broken, and both Israel and Judah went into captivity. The Jews were conquered by Babylon during the days of the Prophet Jeremiah who warned them what was going to happen.

> Jeremiah 11:10 They are turned back to the iniquities of their forefathers, which refused to hear my words; and they went after other gods to serve them: **the house of Israel and the house of Judah have broken my covenant which I made with their fathers.**
>
> Jeremiah 11:11 Therefore thus saith the LORD, Behold, I will bring evil upon them, which they shall not be able to escape; and **though they shall cry unto me, I will not hearken unto them.**

Jeremiah is known as the "Weeping Prophet". Along with the book named after him, he also wrote "Lamentations" which means to grieve or weep. It was a very sad time in Israel during the days of his prophecy.

However, Jeremiah's message wasn't all doom and gloom. Jeremiah also prophesied of the New Covenant. God says this Covenant is not like the one that He made with Moses.

Jeremiah 31:31 Behold, the days come, saith the LORD, that I will make **a new covenant** with the house of Israel, and with the house of Judah:

Jeremiah 31:32 **Not according to the covenant that I made with their fathers** in the day that I took them by the hand to bring them out of the land of Egypt; which my covenant they brake, although I was an husband unto them, saith the LORD:

In the New Covenant, God puts His law into the hearts of His people. Also, everyone who is part of the New Covenant "Knows God and He Knows them". This means God has a personal relationship with them.

Jeremiah 31:33 But this shall be the covenant that I will make with the house of Israel; After those days, saith the LORD, **I will put my law in their inward parts,** and write it in their hearts; and will be their God, and they shall be my people.

Jeremiah 31:34 And they shall teach no more every man his neighbour, and every man his brother, saying, Know the LORD: for **they shall all know me, from the least of them unto the greatest of them,** saith the LORD: for I will forgive their iniquity, and I will remember their sin no more.

God also says this Covenant is an Everlasting Covenant. This means it will not be broken! It is Eternal!

Jeremiah 32:40 And **I will make an everlasting covenant with them**, that I will not turn away from them, to do them good; but **I will put my fear in their hearts, that they shall not depart from me.**

Ezekial also prophesies of the Everlasting Covenant. God says through Ezekial that Israel broke the Covenant (the one given to Moses), but He then tells them that He is going to establish an Everlasting Covenant with them.

> Ezekiel 16:59 For thus saith the Lord GOD; I will even deal with thee as thou hast done, which hast despised the oath **in breaking the covenant.**
>
> Ezekiel 16:60 Nevertheless I will remember my covenant with thee in the days of thy youth, and **I will establish unto thee an everlasting covenant.**

God also says though Ezekial, that the Everlasting Covenant will be a Covenant of Peace.

> Ezekiel 37:26 Moreover I will make **a covenant of peace** with them; **it shall be an everlasting covenant** with them: and I will place them, and multiply them, and will set my sanctuary in the midst of them for evermore.

We are shown in Isaiah that this Covenant of Peace will not be removed. God promises that the mountain and hills will depart and be removed before His kindness is removed from those in this Covenant.

> Isaiah 54:10 For the mountains shall depart, and the hills be removed; but <u>my kindness shall not depart from thee</u>, **neither shall the covenant of my peace be removed**, saith the LORD that hath mercy on thee.

The Covenant promises Everlasting Kindness & Mercy from God.

Isaiah 54:8 In a little wrath I hid my face from thee for a moment; but **with everlasting kindness will I have mercy on thee**, saith the LORD thy Redeemer.

Everyone in this Covenant is also personally taught or guided by the Lord.

Isaiah 54:13 And **all thy children shall be taught of the LORD**; and great shall be the peace of thy children.	John 6:45 **It is written in the prophets, And they shall be all taught of God.** Every man therefore that hath heard, and hath learned of the Father, cometh unto me.

You may say that God says the Everlasting Covenant is with Israel. Well, it is, but when we are Born Again through Faith in Jesus, we as Children of God are grafted into true Israel or as Paul says the "Israel of God". Ezekial also prophesied of the "strangers" receiving inheritance in the land. This was strictly forbidden in the Covenant with Moses. He also says that the "Stranger" would be just like the natural-born Israelite.

Ezekiel 47:22 And it shall come to pass, that ye shall divide it by lot for an inheritance unto you, and to **the strangers that sojourn among you**, which shall beget children among you: and **they shall be unto you as born in the country among the children of Israel**; <u>**they shall have inheritance with you among the tribes of Israel.**</u>

This was a huge mystery and still is to the Jews because in their minds the land was only for the physical descendants of Jacob. God revealed this mystery to Paul and showed him that this is fulfilled in the Gentile members of Christ's Church.

> Ephesians 3:3 How that by revelation **he made known unto me the mystery**; (as I wrote afore in few words,
>
> Ephesians 3:6 **That the Gentiles should be fellowheirs**, and of the same body, **and partakers of his promise in Christ by the gospel:**

Paul also shows us that God's promises in the Everlasting Covenant, are according to Faith. Because of this, God's promises are Sure to the Believer. In other words, we don't have to hope that we are measuring up to the Law in order to receive our inheritance, but we can know that we are Children of God through Faith in Jesus. Also, Paul wants to make clear that we are also spiritual children of Abraham.

> Romans 4:13 For the promise, that he should be the heir of the world, was not to Abraham, or to his seed, through the law, **but through the righteousness of faith.**
>
> Romans 4:16 **Therefore it is of faith, that it might be by grace**; to the end the promise might be **sure to all the seed**; not to that only which is of the law, but to that also which is of **the faith of Abraham; who is the father of us all,**

The Covenant with Moses was dedicated by blood. An animal was killed, and its blood was sprinkled on the people. This was a picture of the New Covenant and the blood of Jesus being sprinkled on us. Shortly before Jesus went to the cross, He told us that His blood was the blood of the New Covenant.

Matthew 26:28 For **this is my blood of the new testament**, which is shed for many for the remission of sins.

God says in Zechariah that it's because of the Blood of Jesus that we are saved from Hell. Another word for Hell in the Bible is the Pit. We were prisoners of the Pit until we were rescued by the Blood of Jesus.

Zechariah 9:11 As for thee also, **by the blood of thy covenant** I have sent forth thy prisoners **out of the pit wherein is no water**.

And so the Lord who is our Great Shepherd, established the Everlasting Covenant through His blood.

Hebrews 13:20 Now the God of peace, that brought again from the dead <u>our Lord Jesus, that great shepherd of the sheep</u>, **through the blood of the everlasting covenant,**

Promises of the Everlasting Covenant:

It is an Everlasting/Eternal Covenant.
It is not in accordance with the Covenant of Moses.
God will put His Law in the hearts of the people.
He will be their God and they will be His people.
Everyone in the Covenant will Know God and He will Know them.
God will forgive their iniquity and remember their sins no more.
God will put His fear in the hearts of the people so they will not depart from Him.
God will give the people Peace, Kindness, and Mercy and promises that none of which will be removed.
God will personally teach and guide all the people.
God promises His Spirit and the testimony of the people will not depart from them.

If you've been Born Again and are in the Everlasting Covenant with God, everything that happens to you will in some way work for your good. But what if it's bad or involves sin you say? In one way or another God will make it benefit you in the long run through teaching and chastisement. Before you think that's an excuse to sin, realize that God is interested more in your spiritual benefit than a physical one. Also, God is more interested in eternity than this physical world that's going to be destroyed.

Romans 8:28 And we know that **all things work together for good to them that love God, to them who are the called** according to his purpose.

You see, if you're Born Again, God foreknew (knew ahead of time) you would believe before you ever believed, and He's been using everything that happens in your life to make you more like Jesus.

Romans 8:29 For **whom he did foreknow, he also did predestinate to be conformed to the image of his Son**, that he might be the firstborn among many brethren.

Moreover, if God foreknew you and predestinated (pre-determined) to make you more like Jesus, He Called you to Himself, He Justified you, and He's going to Glorify you. This is an unbroken chain. All those who He foreknew would believe will be glorified!

Romans 8:30 Moreover whom he did predestinate, them he also called: and whom he called, them he also justified: and whom he justified, **them he also glorified**.

If God died for us when we were sinners and His enemies to save us, how much more will He not use His power to keep us saved?

Romans 5:8 But God commendeth his love toward us, in that, while we were yet sinners, Christ died for us.
Romans 5:9 **Much more then, being now justified by his blood, we shall be saved from wrath through him**.
Romans 5:10 For if, when we were enemies, we were reconciled to God by the death of his Son, **much more, being reconciled, we shall be saved by his life.**

Paul understood the promises of the Everlasting Covenant. It's because of these promises that we can be sure that our Salvation is secure. If someone thinks a truly Born-Again person can lose their Salvation, they need to think about how they would lose it. Will they lose it because they fail to keep the Law? That won't work because keeping the Law is not part of this Covenant. What if they leave Christ? Well, God has promised to keep us from doing that, so if you leave Christ, you were never a part of the Covenant to begin with. We stay saved the same way we got saved which is Trusting in the Blood of Jesus and God has promised to keep us in His love. Because of God's promises, Paul understood that nothing can separate us from God's love.

Romans 8:31 What shall we then say to these things? **If God be for us, who can be against us?**

Romans 8:32 He that spared not his own Son, but delivered him up for us all, how shall he not with him also freely give us all things?

Romans 8:33 Who shall lay any thing to the charge of God's elect? **It is God that justifieth.**

Romans 8:**38 For I am persuaded, that neither death, nor life, nor angels, nor principalities, nor powers, nor things present, nor things to come,**

Romans 8:**39 Nor height, nor depth, nor any other creature, shall be able to separate us from the love of God, which is in Christ Jesus our Lord.**

<u>A list of things that are unable to separate Believers from God's Love:</u>

<u>Death:</u> When you die, you won't be separated from God

<u>Life:</u>   Nothing in your life will separate you from God

<u>Angels:</u> No Angel can separate you from God, this includes Satan

<u>Principalities:</u> No prince, chief, king, president (includes angelic rulers)

<u>Powers:</u> No demonic power or witchcraft, or earthy power

<u>Things Present</u>: Nothing happening in your present life

<u>Things to Come:</u> Nothing that will happen to you in the future

<u>Height:</u> Nothing in Heaven above will separate you from God's love

<u>Depth:</u> Nothing in Hell can separate you from God's love

<u>No other Creature:</u> Anything you can imagine that wasn't mentioned prior can separate you from God's love

Remember, saved people have always been saved by Faith. God told Moses that the people would forsake Him and break the Covenant, after which He would forsake them. However, God had a different message for Joshua. God knew that Joshua was a true Believer and so God told Moses to tell Joshua that He would never fail or forsake him. God also spoke this to Joshua directly.

Deuteronomy 31:6 Be strong and of a good courage, fear not, nor be afraid of them: for the LORD thy God, he it is that doth go with thee; **he will not fail thee, nor forsake thee.**	Joshua 1:5 There shall not any man be able to stand before thee all the days of thy life: as I was with Moses, so I will be with thee: **I will not fail thee, nor forsake thee.**

The word "Forsake" means to totally turn away from something and to abandon it. God promises that when a person is Saved through Faith, He will never Forsake them. Another promise of the Everlasting Covenant is that God will Never Forsake us.

> Hebrews 13:5 Let your conversation be without covetousness; and be content with such things as ye have: for he hath said, **I will never leave thee, nor forsake thee.**

Now, I have a Secret to tell you. It's not actually my Secret. God had a Secret that was only revealed to certain people. This Secret started in the Garden of Eden. When a person feared God and was willing to trust in Him, He gave them a Secret Message. He gave this Message to Adam, Enoch, Noah, Abraham, Job, Moses, Ruth, David, Esther, and many more. This Message was the Secret to Salvation. It was the Message of a Covenant.

> Psalm 25:14 The **secret of the LORD** is with them that fear him; and **he will shew them his covenant**.

The Message that was given to them was the Gospel of Christ. He told them that Salvation was by Grace through Faith in Christ. Christ hadn't yet come, but they were looking for Him and waiting for Him. Everyone who has ever found Salvation has found it the exact same way. There will be no one in Heaven who will be there because they followed the Law. Everyone you'll meet in Heaven will have the same Testimony. They will tell you how they were sinners who deserved Hell but were Saved by the Blood of Jesus.

Throughout time, God gave further revelation regarding the Covenant. They knew the Redeemer was coming but they didn't know when or how. So, God told Abraham that Christ would come from his descendants. Then, it was revealed Christ would come through Isaac, then Jacob, then Judah, and then David. Finally, when the time was right Jesus was born into the world and died for us all. At this point, God's Secret which He had kept since the beginning of the world was revealed.

Romans 16:25 Now to him that is of power to stablish you according to my gospel, and the preaching of Jesus Christ, according to the revelation of the mystery, **which was kept secret since the world began,**

Sin can take the joy of our Salvation away at times. David lost his joy for a short time, but he never lost his salvation.

Psalm 51:11 Cast me not away from thy presence; and take not thy holy spirit from me.
Psalm 51:12 **Restore unto me the joy of thy salvation**; and uphold me with thy free spirit.

Although David felt like the Lord should, He never took His Spirit away from David. If you've been Born Again, God will never take His Spirit away from you either.

1 Samuel 16:13 Then Samuel took the horn of oil, and anointed him in the midst of his brethren: and **the Spirit of the LORD came upon David from that day forward.** So Samuel rose up, and went to Ramah.

David was a model of what a modern-day Christian is. David Trusted in the Lord with all his heart. When David sinned, God showed him mercy in ways that He hadn't shown mercy to other people. God made an Everlasting Covenant with David. As Christians, God has made an Everlasting Covenant with us as well. David said that this Covenant is all his Salvation. David also said the Covenant is Sure.

> 2 Samuel 23:5 Although my house be not so with God; yet **he hath made with me an everlasting covenant**, ordered in all things, **and sure: for this is all my salvation**, and all my desire, although he make it not to grow.

Like David, the Everlasting Covenant is all our Salvation as well. If you're a part of this Covenant you have EVERYTHING! If you're a part of this Covenant, your Salvation is Sure and Certain! The Eternal Security of the Believer is a Biblical Fact. We are Saved by the Lord and His Blood. We are kept Saved by the Lord and His Blood. He has promised that He's going to see our Salvation through to the end and take us Home. This is the Everlasting Covenant and the Sure Mercies of David.

> Isaiah 55:3 Incline your ear, and come unto me: hear, and your soul shall live; and **I will make an everlasting covenant with you, even the sure mercies of David.**